THE ESTABLISHMENT OF THE THIRTEEN COLONIES

DON NARDO

LUCENT BOOKS

A part of Gale, Cengage Learning

GALE
CENGAGE Learning

Detroit • New York • San Francisco • New Haven, Conn • Waterville, Maine • London

LIBRARY OF CONGRESS CATALOGING-IN-PUBLICATION DATA

Nardo, Don, 1947-
  The establishment of the thirteen colonies / by Don Nardo.
    p. cm. -- (The Lucent library of historical eras)
  Includes bibliographical references and index.
  ISBN 978-1-4205-0267-1 (hardcover)
  1. United States--History--Colonial period, ca. 1600-1775--Juvenile iterature. I. Title.
  E188.N365 2010
  973.2--dc22

                                                        2009045055

Lucent Books
27500 Drake Rd.
Farmington Hills, MI 48331

ISBN-13: 978-1-4205-0267-1
ISBN-10: 1-4205-0267-0

Printed in the United States of America
2 3 4 5 6 7 14 13 12 11 10

Printed by Bang Printing, Brainerd, MN, 2nd Ptg.,10/2010

Contents

Foreword

Looking back from the vantage point of the present, history can be viewed as a myriad of intertwining roads paved by human events. Some paths stand out—broad highways whose mileposts, even from a distance of centuries, are clear. The events that propelled the rise to power of Germany's Third Reich, its role in World War II, and its eventual demise, for example, are well defined and documented.

Other roads are less distinct, their route sometimes hidden from view. Modern legislatures may have developed from old tribal councils, for example, but the links between them are indistinct in places, open to discussion and interpretation.

The architecture of civilization—law, religion, art, science, and government—as well as the more everyday aspects of our culture—what we eat, what we wear—all developed along the historical roads and byways. In that progression can be traced every facet of modern life.

A broad look back along these roads reveals that many paths—though of vastly different character—seem to converge at a few critical junctions. These intersections are those great historical eras that echo over the long, steady course of human history, extending beyond the past and into the present.

These epic periods of time are the focus of Historical Eras. They shine through the mists of history like beacons, illuminated by a burst of creativity that propels events forward—so bright that we, from thousands of years away, can clearly see the chain of events leading to the present.

Each Historical Eras consists of a set of books that highlight various aspects of these major eras. For example, the Elizabethan England library features volumes on Queen Elizabeth I and her court, Elizabethan theater, the great playwrights, and everyday life in Elizabethan London.

The mini-library approach allows for the division of each era into its most significant and most interesting parts and the exploration of those parts in depth. Also, social and cultural trends as well as illustrative documents and eyewitness accounts can be prominently featured in individual volumes.

Historical Eras presents a wealth of information to young readers. The lively narrative, fully documented primary and secondary source quotations, maps, photographs, sidebars, and annotated bibliographies serve as launching points for class discussion and further research.

In studying the great historical eras, students also develop a better understanding of our own times. What we learn from the past and how we apply it in the present may shape the future and may determine whether our era will be a guiding light to those traveling future roads.

Introduction

CREATING NEW AND EXCEPTIONAL SOCIETIES

Looking back at the establishment of the North American colonies that later came together to form the United States, one is struck by a number of factors that ensured their growth and ultimate success. First, the people who founded these colonies were determined to be successful in what they called the "New World." Some came to escape religious persecution. Others came because they were destitute and hoped to make a fresh start. Meanwhile other people made the journey to exploit the continent's vast natural resources for markets back in Europe.

In addition to determination, another quality that most of the initial settlers shared was a strong work ethic. At least at first, the vast majority of settlers were agrarians, farmers who made their livings off the land and the plants and animals that inhabited it. "The key to an agrarian culture," scholar Herbert Applebaum points out:

> is an ethic that recognizes the importance of hard, physical labor within a framework of yearly cycles of tasks. Production of agricultural products involves a complex relationship between the actual cultivation of crops and the farmer's cultural values. . . . Visits with friends and relatives, even life-cycle events such as marriages and baptisms, had to be fitted into the agricultural work schedule. . . . At markets and fairs, in newspapers and almanacs, [and] in face-to-face relationships at grinding mills or warehouses, farmers reaffirmed a traditional relationship between crops and work culture. A farming mentality developed [and] a farmer's

ideology and values were in large part bound up with his daily work experience. In colonial America, the work ethic of the farmer was an important ingredient in the cultural values of American society.[1]

A Remarkable Diversity

The most crucial and far-reaching factor that contributed to the success of the settlers and the societies they created was a remarkable diversity in the types of people who came to North America. The people came not from a single European country or county, but from many. Also, there were African slaves who came involuntarily. And all of those outsiders who landed in North America found Native Americans, also frequently called Indians, already inhabiting the continent.

The interactions of these often profoundly different peoples were at first difficult and at times even violent. But in the long run, their variety of customs, ideas, talents, and experiences became the foundation for societies considerably stronger and more flexible than any Europe had ever seen. According to Pulitzer Prize–winning historian Alan Taylor:

The biggest difference [between the colonies and their mother countries] was the unprecedented mixing of radically diverse peoples—African, European, and Indian—under circumstances

A group of Native American men watch boatloads of settlers approach American shores.

stressful for all. The colonial mixing of peoples—and of microbes, plants, and animals from different continents—was unparalleled in speed and volume in global history. Everyone had to adapt to a dramatic new world wrought by those combinations. In their adaptions to, and borrowings from, one another, they created truly exceptional societies (which is not to say that they were either better or worse than European societies, just new and different).[2]

Different Backgrounds and Languages

The diversity of peoples and cultures in the new colonies was much greater than it might have appeared on the surface. Indeed, it encompassed more than a division into a mere three groups—Europeans, Africans, and Indians. In the era in which the first North American colonies arose, European nations and peoples were more insulated from and culturally dissimilar to one another than they are today. Even the residents of the same country could be highly diverse and culturally unalike. "Both the Londoner and rural peasant of Cornwall, in far western England, were English subjects of the same king," writes Taylor, "but they could barely understand one another."[3]

Moreover, even a single colony could contain a wide array of peoples with different backgrounds, customs, and languages. In the 1600s and 1700s, for

Settlers in New Amsterdam were extremely diverse in the 1600s. They included the Dutch, French, Swedes, Germans, as well as many others.

example, some British colonies had a liberal mix of English, Irish, Scots, Dutch, Germans, Swedes, and French. New Amsterdam (later New York) was even more diverse. "Eighteen languages were spoken on Manhattan Island as early as 1646," one expert points out. "The Dutch, Flemish, Walloons, French, Danes, Norwegians, Swedes, English, Scots, Irish, Germans, Poles, Bohemians, Portuguese, and Italians were among the settlement's early inhabitants."[4]

Similarly, the Native American peoples whom the colonists encountered lived in very different physical environments, made their livings in different ways, and spoke markedly different languages. In those days, a much larger cultural rift separated a forest people like the Massachusett from Plains people like the Arapaho (after the introduction of the horse) than separated an English person from a French person. The same cultural diversity existed in Africa. The languages of many West African peoples whom the whites threw together on colonial plantations differed far more from one another than English did from Spanish.

A Whole Greater than Its Parts

In all this diversity and the distrust, arguments, and fighting that long went with it lurked the potential for something unique and monumental. It was, in the end, a multifaceted whole that was greater than any one, or two, or three of its parts. Eventually, that whole, the infant United States, emerged from the colonial experience. At first, despite Thomas Jefferson's statement (in the Declaration of Independence) that all people were equal, the nation's inhabitants were far from it. Most blacks were still slaves. Indians were driven from their ancestral lands and forced onto desolate reservations. And women were second-class citizens who could not vote.

Yet the political ideas and institutions that had developed in the original colonies came together to produce the U.S. Constitution. And this remarkable document made all the difference. Over time, the lofty ideals it represents, coupled with the nation's ability to revise and improve it, allowed one social group after another to achieve full civil rights. The result was a nation that today, though it still struggles to improve lingering defects, is the freest and strongest in human history. Born out of an unprecedented convergence of human diversity, this was the enormous and eventful legacy bequeathed by colonial America to the modern world.

Chapter One

THE NATIVE AMERICANS BEFORE COLONIZATION

Many modern books say that Christopher Columbus and various other European explorers "discovered" the Americas in the late 1400s and early 1500s. But many Native Americans have objected to this statement. And to press the point, in September 1973 Adam Nordwall, chief of the Red Lake Chippewa tribe (based in Minnesota), flew to Italy (Columbus's homeland) and claimed it for all American Indian peoples. "What right had Columbus to 'discover' America," Nordwall asked Italian reporters covering his arrival, "when it was already inhabited for thousands of years? The same right that I have to come to Italy and claim to have discovered your country."[5]

Although some Italians resented Nordwall's audacious publicity stunt, the full weight of modern archaeology supports him. Excavators have found abundant evidence that shows Native Americans discovered the Americas thousands of years before Columbus was born. Indeed, when the first European settlers arrived in North America in the early 1600s, they found the land already occupied by native peoples. The story of how those peoples got there and created a civilization is the crucial preamble to the colonies founded by the British and other Europeans. This long and eventful earlier phase of American history is referred to variously as the "precontact" period (meaning before contact with white culture) and the "precolonial" era.

The Great Migrations

When Native Americans and European colonists did make first contact in North America, one of the key areas where it occurred was the northeastern seaboard, particularly in what are now Massachusetts and Virginia. This would later form the core of Britain's American colonies, which themselves would eventually morph into the infant United States. The exact manner in which Indian peoples colonized this region is not yet known. But archaeologists, anthropologists, and other scholars have pieced together a likely scenario based on archaeological finds and other data collected from across North America.

The first major incident in the peopling of the continent was a natural event that took place in faraway Alaska. Today a wide expanse of ocean called the Bering Strait separates Alaska from Asia. But about 75,000 years ago, during the last major Ice Age, sea levels dropped, exposing a stretch of land that joined the two continents. Scholars call it Beringia, or the Bering Land Bridge.

Because it was a subarctic wilderness, Beringia was very cold and had few trees. But evidence shows that by about 18,000 years ago (16,000 B.C.) it had enough small plants, grasses, and freshwater rivers and ponds to sustain small populations of large animals. These included mammoths (large elephant-like creatures), ground sloths 20 feet (6m) long, beavers the size of black bears, and bison

The Bering Strait, shown here, used to have a stretch of land joining North America and Asia. It is thought the first natives crossed this land bridge to enter America.

with horns 6 feet (1.8m) long. There were also reindeer, horses, camels, bears, mountain lions, and wolves.

Many of these animal species originated in northwestern Asia, in what is now Siberia, and migrated across Beringia into North America.

It was only natural, then, that some of the primitive humans who hunted these creatures in Siberia would follow them across the land bridge. Excavations of very old campsites and human remains show that sometime between fifteen and eleven thousand years ago, a series of

The Deadly Atlatl

The early Native Americans who discovered North America used a deadly hunting weapon called an atlatl. (The term *atlatl* is the name given to it by the Aztec Indians of central Mexico. Stone Age hunters across the world had a wide range of names for it, but modern experts came to use the Aztec term for all of them.) A throwing stick about 18 inches (46cm) long, an atlatl had a wooden handle and a wooden socket or groove into which a hunter placed a premade arrow-like shaft. He then used a forceful overhand motion to send the shaft flying toward the intended target. This weapon produced significantly more forward momentum than the hunter could achieve with his arm alone. So the shaft traveled farther than a spear and struck the target with considerable force. Even a mammoth, a giant elephant-like creature that roamed the early American wilderness, could be killed by an atlatl. Digging at a site in Arizona, modern excavators found the remains of a mammoth that had been killed by Stone Age Indians wielding atlatls.

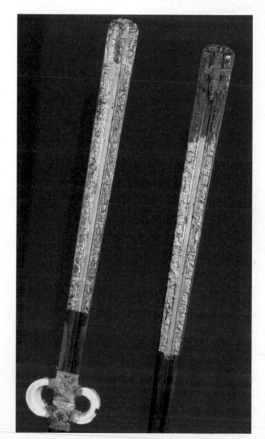

An atlatl, an early Native American hunting weapon.

migrations took place. Bands of hunter-gatherers made their way from Siberia into what are now Alaska and Canada.

If all members of these groups of hunters had stayed in those bleak northern expanses, the history of the Americas would have been very different. However, in each succeeding generation some members moved on. And in this way the migrations relentlessly continued southward and southeastward, although the people involved did not necessarily set out to find new lands. Scholar Philip Kopper explains:

> The term "migration" mistakenly implies intentional relocation, when actually the pace might have been so slow that each generation of immigrants thought they were simply moving to the next overlook or game-rich valley. When they moved deliberately, it may have been to follow a herd of caribou on its annual migration. When they explored, it may have been to discover where the flocks of waterfowl nested or wintered. . . . These first Americans may have lingered wherever they could make a living, which, before the rise of agriculture, meant where they found game. Even staying put, if the leader of a tribe moved his sleeping pallet only by the width of a bed each night, he would find himself ten miles away in a generation, or the distance from Canada to Nebraska in a millennium.[6]

This map shows the locations of Native American tribes, including the Iroquois and Algonquin, in the Eastern Woodlands.

People of the Northeastern Woodlands

As the early hunters spread out across the continent, a few small bands evolved into many peoples and tribes. And as they settled in diverse geographical regions, each having its own local terrain, climate, plants, and animals, they developed different traditions, customs, and languages. Some continued to rely mostly on hunting and gathering, while others learned to grow crops. Not long after agriculture developed in the Old

World (in the Middle East in about 9000 B.C.), it appeared in parts of North America as well. And by about 1000 B.C. (3,000 years ago), the farming of maize (corn), squash, beans, and pumpkins was common in northeastern North America.

Modern experts call that region, which was originally settled by migrating Native Americans in the 8000s B.C., the Northeastern Woodlands. It stretched from the Atlantic coast westward to the eastern shores of the Great Lakes. It encompassed what are now the New England states (Maine, New Hampshire, Vermont, Massachusetts, Rhode Island, and Connecticut), New York, Pennsylvania, New Jersey, and coastal Virginia. Large parts of this area consisted of low, heavily forested mountain ranges and numerous lakes and rivers. All across the region game was abundant, soils were rich, and the climate was fairly moderate. Under these hospitable conditions, many different Indian peoples adjusted to individual geographical niches (mountains, river valleys, coastal plains, and so on) and thrived.

Although each had its local customs, most of these northeastern peoples belonged to two larger cultural and linguistic groups—the Iroquois and the Algonquin. Each was divided into many separate tribes or groups of tribes who spoke dialects of either the Iroquoian or Algonquian mother tongue. Most tribes in New England were Algonquin. They included the Narragansett in Rhode Island, the Massachusett and Wampano-

ag in Massachusetts, and the Micmac in Maine. Among other Algonquin tribes in the northeast were the Montauk in Long Island (now in southeastern New York) and the Delaware (in what is now the state named for them). Some of the Iroquois tribes in the northeast included the Mohawk and Seneca in western and central New York and the Tuscarora, who originally lived in southern Virginia.

Caretakers of the Land

As these groups settled into their local regions, they learned to adapt to the climate of that region. Members of each tribe also learned about the plants and animals in the area. They found the best ways to hunt and trap the animals, as well as how to gather certain plants and grow others.

These are the very same adjustments and survival techniques that European settlers would later employ in these regions. And an examination of the ways in which the Indians settled the land shows how their approach differed markedly from that of white colonists. First, most Native American groups had no concept of land ownership, whereas white settlers came from societies in which land ownership was a major pillar of family and social relationships. Typically, Indians believed that they were merely using lands provided to any and all peoples by nature or a divine creator (often translated by whites as the "Great Spirit").

Also, most Native Americans had little or no interest in conquering other peo-

Native Americans, like this Iroquois warrior, found the best ways to utilize the land, hunting animals and growing crops.

inhabited New England, including Massachusetts, where Europeans eventually established the pivotal Plymouth and Massachusetts Bay colonies. When the Algonquin first settled this area, their initial priority was to find reliable food supplies. They saw that deer, beavers, rabbits, and other game, along with fish, clams, and other marine animals, were plentiful in the region. So they made their livings in large part by hunting and fishing. Archaeological evidence indicates that they became experts at these activities and thereby maintained an extremely diverse and wholesome diet. In the remains of just one village inhabited by members of the Massachusett tribe, anthropologists discovered evidence of food sources that include bear, deer, beaver, fox, mink, blue heron, mallard duck, harbor seal, hawk, eagle, scallop, snapping turtle, clam, snail, sea bass, stingray, and many others.

It is important to note that the tribe did not overhunt or overfish, which would have quickly depleted these valuable resources. This might have happened if the villagers had constantly tried to expand their territory and population. However, the Massachusett and other northeastern tribes almost always maintained stable numbers and lived within the natural carrying capacity of their individual territories. (The carrying capacity of a species or human group is the number of individuals that species or group can continually sustain, given the food, water, and other resources available in its environment.)

ples in order to take and hold their lands, which was a common practice in the Old World. Instead, they sought to do the best they could in their own niches. And for the most part, they respected the status quo and traditional balance between nature and humans and between tribes. Thus, the tendency among the northeastern Indians was to find a vacant area and settle it, but thereafter to act more as a caretaker of that area than as an owner.

A clear example of this approach is the manner in which the so-called southern Algonquin utilized the lands they settled. Several of the southern Algonquin tribes

The Iroquois Longhouse

In contrast to the Algonquin, whose trademark lodging was the wigwam, the Iroquois built larger, more elaborate dwellings called longhouses. The average longhouse was 50 to 100 feet (15m to 30m) long, and some were up to 300 feet (91m) long, the length of a football field. The longhouses had a semicircular arched ceiling resting atop two vertical walls. The Iroquois used freshly cut saplings for the structure's frame. They forced the bottoms of these young trees firmly into the ground and bent over their tops to form the curved ceiling, then covered this framework with thick layers of elm bark. Often the Iroquois built rows of longhouses, not only to create a close-knit community, but also for mutual protection. Further protection for the entire village came from a sturdy stockade, a wooden wall made by lashing many small and medium-size tree trunks tightly together.

Iroquois longhouses.

Wigwams, made from saplings, were common homes for Algonquin peoples.

Algonquin Society

The Massachusett were also farmers. To supplement their hunting, fishing, and foraging, they grew corn, beans, and squash. They traded some of these items, as well as beaver pelts, deerskins, handmade jewelry, and herbs used in healing, with neighboring tribes, who in turn traded with groups farther away. Soon a complex trading network developed across the northeast.

Decisions about land use, what and with whom to trade, and other important matters had to be made in each village or tribal unit. So each village or tribe had a head man or chief-like official. Anthropologist Kathleen Bragdon explains:

Like most of their neighbors, the Massachusett were organized into

political units known as *sachemships*, each led by a hereditary ruler, usually male, known as a *sachem* or *sagamore*. A complex and hierarchical [ladderlike] social order was characteristic of these sachemships, with the sachem occupying the position of highest prestige. The sachem's responsibilities included the allocation of land, diplomacy, trade, and decisions concerning warfare. The sachem's advisors, sometimes called "nobles" by English settlers, shared the burdens of leadership as well. Warriors who underwent rigorous training also occupied positions of status within Massachusett society.[7]

No matter how high or low one's prestige in Algonquin society, he or she lived in the same kind of dwelling as everyone else. (This was another difference between the Indians and whites; the latter tended to put great store in personal wealth, and those who had more of it lived in bigger, more comfortable homes than those who had less.) The characteristic and most common kind of house among southern Algonquin was called a wigwam. (This term was later used rather indiscriminately by white people to describe almost any Indian home, but technically it applies only to Algonquin houses.) A typical wigwam could be built in a single day by just a few people. It was usually oval shaped and made from saplings forced into the ground, bent into arches, and tied together with plant fibers. One expert writes:

> The resultant frame was covered with large bark strips . . . leaving a smoke hole in the center and one end open for a doorway, which was covered with a hide or a woven rush [reed] mat. . . . The finished structure could be up to 20 feet long and 14 feet wide, with walls 6 or 7 feet high and an overall height of 14 feet at the arch. The sleeping areas were arranged around the central fire and consisted of mats or cedar boughs and animal skins. A storage area was established at

America's First Democracy?

Some modern scholars think that the Iroquois had a political system that featured some of the same democratic elements the U.S. Constitution eventually did. Evidence shows that five of the major Iroquois tribes, all based in what is now New York State, came together in a major and long-lasting political alliance that the whites called the Iroquois Confederacy. It had a sort of constitution, consisting of a set of legal rules and procedures, which still survives. It calls for disputes to be arbitrated by deliberation, discussion, and ultimately democratic voting among the member tribes. If an important issue or question arose, representatives from two of the five tribes discussed it. Then the representatives from two other member tribes reviewed and discussed it. Finally, the representatives from the fifth tribe looked at the arguments of the two other groups and made a final judgment. In a sense, therefore, the fifth tribe played a similar role to that of the U.S. vice president. In his job as president of the Senate, the vice president can break a tie vote among opposing factions of senators.

Native Americans often lived with their extended family—grandmothers and uncles—with each person performing different duties.

the rear of the structure. Woodland peoples used the wigwam for sleeping, for storing possessions, and as an escape from inclement weather.[8]

Also characteristic of the tribes who lived near the Plymouth and Massachusetts Bay colonies (including the Nauset, Wampanoag and Pokanoket, as well as the Massachusett) was the extended family unit. It consisted not only of a father, mother, and children, but also of grandparents, aunts, and other close relatives. This arrangement allowed several individuals from different generations to share in nurturing and educating the children. There were no formal schools. Rather, women taught young girls to make clothes and plant and harvest crops. And men showed young boys how to build wigwams, hunt, fish, and fight. Children also learned about life, the world around them, and the proper ways to treat both other people and the land by hearing their elders tell stories about their ancestors, the Great Spirit, animals, and how all of these interacted within the environment. Most of these tales were informative, colorful, and positive in tone.

The Coming of the Whites

In later times, however, Indian storytellers also passed on bitter laments and warnings. They looked back on the first contacts between Native Americans and whites with sadness and regret and portrayed the coming of the white colonists as the beginning of the end of traditional Indian cultures. In 1788 after years of dealing with the colonists' attempts to conquer or eradicate local tribes, one leading Algonquin told his people:

There is no faith to be placed in [the whites'] words. They are not like the Indians, who are only enemies while at war and are friends in peace. They will say to an Indian, "My friend! My brother!" They will take him by the hand, and at the same moment destroy him. . . . Remember! That this day I have warned you to beware of such friends as these.[9]

Chapter Two

THE FIRST EUROPEANS TO SEE NORTH AMERICA

Although it was early Native Americans who actually discovered North America, the first Europeans to see the continent certainly viewed themselves as its discoverers. These voyagers and explorers came from many different nations and regions. And their sightings and/or landings in the Americas occurred over the course of several centuries. Few of these pioneers managed to establish colonies in North America and none of those colonies turned out to be permanent. Nevertheless, these early explorations laid the necessary groundwork for the widespread colonization of the Americas that soon followed.

All of these events were part of a momentous turning point in world history. For the first time, Europeans expanded their horizons outward to see the entire world, of which they occupied only a small part. And rising to the challenge, they exploited the economic potential that control of the vast resources of the Americas could bring. "Long a barrier to Europeans," historian Alan Taylor writes.

the Atlantic became their highway to distant lands, [where] the mariners established fortified outposts to dominate local trade, creating the first transoceanic global empires. It was an extraordinary and unprecedented burst of geographic understanding, daring, and enterprise. [By] enriching Europe, the new resources financed further exploration and conquest [and the] exploitation of the Americas [transformed] Europe from a parochial [narrow-minded] backwater into the world's most dynamic and powerful continent.[10]

The Norse Prelude

This enormous economic and in many ways political, military, and intellectual transformation occurred mainly between the late 1400s and late 1600s. Many modern books refer to it as the "great age of discovery" or words to that effect. However, the explorers and adventurers of that pivotal era were not the first Europeans to sight and set foot in the Americas. That distinction goes to the Norse, better known as the Vikings. A hardy, daring, seafaring folk, they hailed from the chilly, mountainous region of Scandinavia, in Europe's northernmost region.

Evidence, including both epic tales passed down through the generations and archaeological finds, shows that in the ninth and tenth centuries Viking explorers and colonizers sailed westward into the northern Atlantic region. They founded thriving colonies in Ireland, Iceland, and Greenland. (In those days, southern Greenland was largely ice free, and the climate was hospitable enough to support farming.)

The southern tip of Greenland lies only a few hundred miles northeast of North America's easternmost territories. So it is perhaps not surprising that sooner or later some enterprising Vikings would run into that continent, which was previously unknown to Europeans. Sometime between A.D. 985

Leif Eriksson stands on his Viking ship as it sails from Greenland to North America.

and 989, a Viking explorer named Bjarni Herjolfsson left one of the Greenland colonies and several days later sighted what is now Newfoundland, in southern Canada. Some scholars think he may also have seen and landed in Labrador, Nova Scotia, and/or Cape Cod (now part of Massachusetts). Herjolfsson did not attempt to establish any colonies. Instead, he sailed back to Greenland and reported what he had seen, which included vast forests filled with game.

This report aroused the interest of other Vikings, who felt that the lands Herjolfsson had witnessed might be ideal for colonization. An expedition commanded by Leif Eriksson reached North America sometime between 998 and 1002. First he reached what is now Canada's Baffin Island. Then he moved on to a land he called "Woodland," which was probably Labrador. Finally Eriksson arrived in a place he called Vinland because of the large number of wild grapes growing there. The exact location of Vinland is still debated by scholars, who variously place it as far north as Newfoundland and Nova Scotia and as far south as Cape Cod and Rhode Island's Narragansett Bay. Wherever it was, Eriksson and his men erected a settlement and spent the winter.

Later, after Eriksson returned to Greenland, his brother, Thorwald, led an expedition that located Leif's camp in Vinland. There, the Vikings encountered some Native Americans, whom they called "Skraelings." A fight ensued, during which Thorwald was killed. Among the Viking expeditions that followed, one led by Thorfinn Karlsefni managed to found a colony that lasted three years, but the colonists abandoned it when the natives attacked in force.

After that, partly because the climate in Greenland was growing colder, no more Viking expeditions tried to reach North America. Nor did any other Europeans launch such voyages of their own, despite the fact that tales of the Vikings' explorations filtered into other parts of Europe. The reasons for this lack of interest remain uncertain. According to New York University scholar Irwin Unger:

> No European monarch fitted out an expedition to claim the new lands and settle them. No merchants pooled their capital to seek profits in the rich, distant country. No crowds of plain folk hurried down to the wharves to board ship for a new life in the western lands. As far as Europe was concerned, it was if the Norse discoveries had never been made.[11]

Columbus Leads the Way

By the time of Christopher Columbus's famous Atlantic voyage almost five hundred years later, Europeans had completely forgotten about the Vikings' voyages. Columbus, an Italian sailing for Spain, never made land-

This map shows the course of Christopher Columbus's exploration of Hispaniola, Cuba, and the Bahamas in 1492.

fall in North America, where English colonial America would later grow and prosper. Instead, he landed in the Bahamas, Hispaniola (now Haiti and the Dominican Republic), Cuba, and other offshore islands. However, his expeditions were important, inspiring countless other explorers, including those who explored what is now the eastern U.S. seaboard.

When Columbus first encountered Native Americans during his initial voyage, he gave them the name "Indians" (which thereafter became the most common term for them). This was because he assumed he had landed in the "Indies," then defined as islands off Asia's eastern coast. His first journal entries about the Indians were purely descriptive. He wrote that they were "a very poor people." Then he added:

> They all go completely naked, even the women [all] whom I saw were young, not above thirty years of age, well made, with fine shapes and faces; their hair short, and coarse like that of a horse's tail, combed toward the forehead, except a small portion which they suffer to hang down behind, and never cut. Some paint themselves with black . . . others with white, others with red, and others with such colors as they can find.[12]

Two days later, however, Columbus had decided that they were inferior and weak and therefore ripe for conquest and enslavement. In his journal he wrote:

> The people here are simple in war-like matters, as your Highnesses [Queen Isabella of Spain] will see by those seven which I have ordered to be taken and carried to Spain in order to learn our language and return, unless your Highnesses should choose to have them all transported to Castile [in Spain], or held captive in the island. I could conquer the whole of them with fifty men, and govern them as I pleased.[13]

Columbus Observes the Natives

In his journal, Christopher Columbus made a number of observations of the native peoples he encountered in the Caribbean region, including this one:

Some paint the face, others the whole body; others only the eyes, and others the nose. Weapons they have none, nor are acquainted with them, for I showed them swords which they grasped by the blades, and cut themselves through ignorance. They have no iron. . . . They are all of good stature and size. . . . It appears to me that the people . . . would be good servants and I am of opinion that they would very readily become Christians, as they appear to have no religion.

Christopher Columbus, "Journal of the First Voyage of Columbus," in *Original Narratives of Early American History: The Northmen, Columbus and Cabot, 985–1503*, eds. Julius E. Olson and Edward Gaylord Bourne. New York: Scribner's, 1906.

In governing these islands, Columbus and his successors were ruthless. The natives were systematically enslaved, tortured, raped, and worked to death. A little more than two decades after Columbus landed in Hispaniola, 80 percent of the island's original 250,000 inhabitants were dead. And by the early 1600s, all had been exterminated.

Exploring North America

Columbus's voyage paved the way for others who wanted to explore or settle in the Americas. At first the majority of the colonizers were Spanish. They included Hernán Cortés, who conquered the Aztecs in Mexico, and Francisco Pizarro, who did the same to the Incas in Peru. By 1600 Spain controlled large portions of Central and South America.

John Cabot leaving England in 1497 to explore North America.

Exploring Coastal Rhode Island

Among the areas that Italian navigator Giovanni da Verrazano investigated during his North American voyage was the coast of what is now Rhode Island. The record of the trip states in part:

We found an excellent harbor [probably lower Narragansett Bay]; before entering it, we saw [some] boats full of people who came around the ship uttering various cries of wonderment. They did not come nearer than fifty paces but stopped to look at the structure of our ship, our persons, and our clothes; then all together they raised a loud cry which meant that they were joyful. We reassured them somewhat by imitating their gestures, and they came near enough for us to throw them a few little bells and mirrors and many trinkets, which they took and looked at, laughing, and then they confidently came on board ship. Among them were two kings, who were as beautiful of stature and build as I can possibly describe. . . . These people are the most beautiful and have the most civil customs that we have found on this voyage. They are taller than we are; they are a bronze color, some tending more toward whiteness, others to a tawny color; the face is clear-cut; the hair is long and black, and they take great pains to decorate it; the eyes are black and alert, and their manner is sweet and gentle.

Quoted in Lawrence C. Wroth, ed., *The Voyages of Giovanni da Verruzzano, 1524–1528.* New Haven, CT: Yale University Press, 1970, p. 137.

As a result, several other European nations concentrated their colonizing efforts in North America. England and France, for instance, made some initial inroads into what are now southeastern Canada and the northeastern United States (then assumed to be part of Asia). In 1496 England's king Henry VII granted explorer John Cabot a written license for an expedition. According to the document, Cabot had permission

to find, discover and investigate whatsoever islands, countries, regions or provinces of heathens and infidels [non-Christians], in whatsoever part of the world placed, which before this time were unknown to all Christians. We have also granted to them and to . . . the heirs and deputies of them . . . license to set up our aforesaid banners and ensigns in any town, city, castle, island or mainland whatsoever, newly found by them. And that the before-mentioned John [Cabot] and his sons or their heirs and deputies may conquer, occupy, and possess whatsoever such towns, castles, cities and islands by them thus discovered.[14]

Early in 1497 Cabot departed England on a single ship and made it safely across the north Atlantic. As the first European to reach North America since the Vikings, he had no idea where he was when he landed. And to this day the spot where he first landed is widely disputed. The best guess of most scholars is that it was somewhere in Newfoundland. Cabot made a second voyage to North America the following year, this time with five ships, but he and his men were never heard from again. Following this expensive disaster, several decades passed before the financially struggling English monarchy felt up to renewing its efforts to find lands suitable for colonization.

In the meantime, France attempted to follow up on Cabot's explorations. As early as 1504, French fishing vessels crossed the ocean and searched the waters of the Grand Banks (the shallow coastal region lying southeast of Newfoundland). Two decades later a French king, Francis I, sent Italian navigator Giovanni da Verrazano to explore the lands bordering the Grand Banks. In April 1524 Verrazano sailed into what is now New York Harbor and saw the Hudson River. Later he journeyed northward along the coasts of Rhode Island, Massachusetts, and Maine. In a letter he sent to King Francis he describes what are now New York, Long Island, and Block Island. He writes:

After a hundred leagues [about 300 miles] we found a very agreeable place between two small but prominent hills; between them a very wide river [the Hudson], deep at its mouth, flows out into the sea; and with the help of the tide, which rises eight feet, any laden ship could have passed from the sea into the river estuary [New York Harbor]. Once we were anchored off the coast and well sheltered . . . we took the small boat up this river to land which we found densely populated. The people were . . . dressed in birds' feathers of various color and they came toward us joyfully, uttering loud cries of wonderment, and showing us [the] safest place to beach the boat. . . . [Soon, however, a storm] blew in from the sea, and we were forced to return to the ship, leaving the land with much regret on account of its favorable conditions and beauty. . . . We weighed anchor, and sailed eastward since the land veered in that direction [along the southern shore of Long Island], and covered 80 leagues, always keeping in sight of land. We discovered a triangular-shaped island [Block Island]. It was full of hills, covered in trees, and highly populated to judge by the fires we saw burning continually along the shore. We [chose not to] anchor there because the weather was unfavorable.[15]

More Europeans followed Cabot and Verrazano into the same region. In 1533 and again in 1535, Frenchman Jacques Cartier explored southern Canada; England's Walter Raleigh landed in what is now North Carolina; and fishing fleets from Portugal, Italy, France, England, and other countries repeatedly moved through the waters along North America's eastern seaboard. However, none of them established any permanent colonies.

A Pleasant and Inviting Land

The person who did the most to pave the way for the first English colonies was English lawyer, trader, and explorer Bartholomew Gosnold. After gaining financial support to establish a colony, Gosnold set out to find a suitable place in 1602. In May of that year, his ship, the *Concord*, with a crew of thirty-two, reached the coast of Maine. Then it sailed southward, eventually landing on a peninsula shaped like a big fishhook. There were so many cod in the nearby waters that Gosnold called the peninsula Cape Cod, the name it still bears. One of Gosnold's crewmen later wrote:

Near this cape we [anchored] in fifteen fathoms [90 feet/27m],

Gosnold Investigates Martha's Vineyard

One of the surviving accounts of Bartholomew Gosnold's voyage along the coast of what is now Massachusetts tells about his sighting and naming of Martha's Vineyard:

We saw an uninhabited island, [and we] named it Martha's Vineyard. . . . The island is five miles [long], and has 41 degrees and one quarter of latitude. The place most pleasant. . . . We went ashore, and found it full of woods, vines, gooseberry bushes, whortleberries, raspberries, eglantines [flowers], etc. Here we had cranes . . . geese, and diverse other birds which there at that time upon the cliffs being sandy with some rocky stones, did breed and have young. In this place we saw deer. Here we rode in eight fathoms [48 feet/15m] near the shore which we took great store of cod—as before at Cape Cod, but much better. [The] next morning offered unto us fast running thirteen savages . . . armed with bows and arrows without any fear. They brought tobacco, deer-skins, and some sodden fish. . . . This island is sound, and has no danger about it.

Quoted in Gabriel Archer, *Gosnold's Settlement at Cuttyhunk*. Boston: Old South Work, 1902, pp. 6–7.

Bartholomew Gosnold trades with a group of Native Americans in Virginia.

where we took [a] great store of codfish, for which we . . . called it Cape Cod. Here we saw sculls of herring, mackerel, and other small fish, in great abundance. This is a low sandy shoal, but without danger [of running aground]. This cape is well near a mile broad. . . . The captain went here ashore and found the ground to be full of peas, strawberries, whortleberries, etc. [Soon] a young Indian came here to the captain, armed with his bow and arrows, and had certain plates of copper hanging at his ears; he showed a willingness to help us in our occasions [pursuits].[16]

Gosnold went on to see and name the island of Martha's Vineyard, and a bit farther south he established a small outpost on Elizabeth Island (now Cuttyhunk Island). That potential colony was abandoned after only a few weeks because of a lack of sufficient food, tools, and other provisions. But lengthy accounts of the voyage by two of Gosnold's crewmen were published and became widely popular in England. They made coastal Massachusetts sound extremely pleasant and inviting and inspired other Englishmen to try to create colonies there. The birth of British colonial America, whose people would eventually transform the world, was close at hand.

Chapter Three

THE COLONIZERS AND THEIR MOTIVES

The people who colonized North America's eastern seaboard in the 1600s came from nearly every corner of Europe, including England, Scotland, France, Holland, Germany, Italy, Sweden, and Poland. They also came from a wide range of back grounds, religions, and professions. Moreover, some were poor, others were rich, and still others were somewhere in between. In addition, some immigrated voluntarily, while others made the trans-Atlantic voyage in chains. In some ways, the early inhabitants of what eventually became British America represented a cross section of the Old World societies.

Yet despite this diversity, the early settlers also fell into a few broad types, categories, and patterns that in the long run shaped the overall character, laws, and customs of the colonies. First, a majority of the colonists were of English extraction, particularly in the New England settlements. And partly for that reason, the overarching culture that developed in colonial America was English speaking and governed by English laws.

Second, most of the immigrants came from the middle and lower-middle classes, whose members made their livings as shopkeepers, craftsmen, and farmers. Hardworking, family oriented, and God fearing, they saw themselves as making up both the heart and backbone of society. Their steadfast qualities may well have been the inspiration for a now-famous remark made by a leading Massachusetts colonist in 1669. He said, "God sifted a whole [Old World] nation that He might bring choice grain over into his [New World] wilderness."[17]

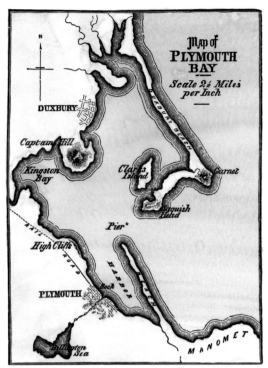

A map of Plymouth Bay, Massachusetts, where William Bradford and a group of settlers colonized and learned to farm the land.

Learning to Be Farmers

Another broad generalization that can be made about the early settlers of North America's eastern seaboard is that most were tied to the land. Despite the presence of some shopkeepers and artisans in the towns, a majority of colonists lived in rural areas and made their livings as farmers. This does not mean that most of the settlers had been farmers in their native lands, however. In fact, many of them learned to farm after they arrived in North America. This seems to differ from a statement made by Wil-

liam Bradford, one of the early organizers and governors of Plymouth Colony, in what is now southeastern Massachusetts. In his famous treatise on the colony, he writes:

> Being thus constrained [forced] to leave their native soil and country, their lands and livings, and all their friends and familiar acquaintances . . . they knew not how [they were going to survive], especially seeing they were not acquainted with trades nor trade (by which that country does subsist) but had only been used to a plain country life, and the innocent trade of husbandry [agriculture].[18]

Abundant evidence shows that Bradford simply got it wrong. It is possible that he based this statement primarily on his personal experiences, since he had been born into an English farming family. However, the backgrounds of most of his fellow travelers on the *Mayflower* were quite different. One leader, John Carver, had been a printer; another, Myles Standish, had been a soldier; and a majority of the others who settled in Massachusetts had originally been craftsmen and shop workers, including shoemakers, carpenters, tailors, weavers, coopers (barrel makers), blacksmiths, and brewers. Historians have determined that only about a quarter of the families in the fledgling Massachusetts Bay Colony had made their livings as farmers in Europe. When one considers the economic hardships a farmer faced in moving his family to the Americas, it becomes clear why few farmers were willing to make the effort, at least initially. Historian Howard S. Russell writes:

> Consider what was involved. Each countryman had to sell or lease his land . . . renouncing cherished ancestral or acquired rights and privileges. He had then to provide himself with tools and equipment for his new enterprise, and to pay the heavy cost of transporting household goods and livestock 3,000 miles. He had to provide in advance supplies for the subsistence of his family, servants, and stock, for many months after arrival.[19]

Another England?

The reasons why various groups and individuals immigrated to North America are much harder to generalize. Indeed, the reasons and motives were many and diverse and often depended on such factors as economic means and social rank. One can start by examining what motivated the minority of settlers who had wealthy, upper-class backgrounds. A number of modern scholars call it "the aristocratic impulse."

Some of these members of the noble class, or landed gentry, looked back on and longed for the medieval days of yore, when a handful of rich feudal lords held sway over thousands of poor agricultural serfs. By the 1600s that society no longer existed in England, although there were

The travelers on the ship Mayflower *were extremely diverse, ranging from soldiers to carpenters to farmers.*

still wealthy landowners with high social rank and political power. Most of them were content to stay put. They had no desire to risk life and limb, brave hardships, and perform menial labor in some faraway unknown land.

But some of their sons saw potential economic, social, and political opportunities in North America. This was particularly true for second, third, and fourth sons, who often did not inherit many honorary titles, nor much land or wealth, from their rich fathers. One scholar writes:

> The New World promised new opportunity and a chance for adventure and glory. Many gentlemen [also] saw it as an opportunity to carve out an estate along with the title, honors, and income they missed at home. Not knowing the realities of the American environment, they expected another England—an England already largely past—where they might live as great landed magnates [lords] surrounded by [admiring] serfs.[20]

This sort of grandiose expectation of power and glory turned out to be mostly a dream. The attempt to install a new aristocracy in North America largely failed, in part because "the character of the emigration created something close to an equal society," writes scholar David F. Hawke. "In economic terms, the distance between the bottom and the top of society was relatively slight." Rich or not, and liking it or not, during a colony's first few years, everyone had to pitch in and work hard. So frequently, would-be landed lords, if they survived the first winters, "sailed home with blistered hands and emaciated bodies, convinced that, for all its faults, a more benign England offered a better way of life,"[21] writes Hawke.

Escaping Persecution

A more common reason for crossing the ocean to North America was to escape religious intolerance and be able to believe and worship as one pleased. All sorts of religious groups were persecuted for a variety of reasons in Europe in late medieval and early modern times. In England most such groups grew out of a volatile situation created by King Henry VIII in the 1530s.

Like the vast majority of his subjects, Henry was at first a Catholic. He had no interest in joining the Protestant movement initiated by German clergyman Martin Luther in 1517. But in 1529, Pope Clement VII refused to annul (declare void) Henry's marriage to Catherine of Aragon, who had failed to bear him a son and male heir. This marked the beginning of a feud between the king and pope that resulted in the emergence of a new Protestant denomination, the Church of England (or Anglican Church) under Henry's daughter, Queen Elizabeth I (who reigned from 1558 to 1603).

Not everyone was happy with this new arrangement. For example, some Catho-

A group of Puritans attempts to flee England to avoid persecution for their religious beliefs.

lics refused to give up their traditional faith and suffered persecution for it. In contrast, other people thought that the new English church had retained too many Catholic beliefs and rituals. They wanted to "purify" the Anglican Church of these elements. So they became known as Puritans. Members of the group brought together an unusual mix of radical and conservative values. Noted historian Samuel E. Morison explains:

The English Puritans were radical in that they proposed to get at the root of everything, no matter what or who stood in their way. But in a

The Colonizers and Their Motives 35

larger sense they were conservative, even reactionary [backward looking], since their aim was to restore "the church unspotted pure" of the early Christians and so reform society that one could lead the New Testament life and at the same time earn a living. They wished [to] get back to apostolic [biblical] times, when the men who had seen Jesus [were] still alive. God, they believed, had dictated the Bible as the complete guide to life.[22]

The Puritans worked to change the system from within. But others who opposed the practices of the Church of England decided to leave the church altogether. This earned them the name "Separatists." One small group of Separatists decided to move to North America, where they could escape persecution and arrest (since being a Separatist was against the law). These were the settlers who founded Plymouth Colony and became known as Pilgrims.

Meanwhile, other radical and persecuted English religious groups headed for the Americas. Among them were the Society of Friends, or Quakers, who believed that God's will and moral values found expression mainly through a believer's own conscience rather than through elaborate rituals and priesthood. At least a few Quakers ended up in nearly all of the British American colonies, although the majority, with the permission of the king, moved to Pennsylvania.

This policy of allowing religious dissenters to settle in the Americas ended up as one of the great strengths of the English colonies as compared to the Spanish and French settlements. Scholar Irwin Unger explains that Spain and France

refused to allow religious dissenters to emigrate to their American possessions. This [policy] seriously limited the number of Europeans who went to the French and Spanish colonies. Eventually, much of the advantage in wealth and population enjoyed by British America over new Spain and new France derived from the more liberal British approach, which preserved the energies and talents of religious dissidents for the advantage of the British Empire. Not only did dissenters help swell the population of the English settlements, they also deeply imprinted their special characteristics upon the new communities. Some of the most energetic and talented people of England and Europe chose to leave their homelands for the "howling wilderness" of America because they could no longer endure the religious harassment at home.[23]

Economic Motives

Although escaping persecution was a frequent reason for moving to North America, the most prevalent motives were economic by far. For a number of people of less-than-average means

Elizabeth Legislates Against the Puritans

In 1593 Queen Elizabeth I signed the Act Against the Puritans, which provided for arrest and imprisonment for such religious dissenters. It reads:

For the preventing and avoiding of such great inconveniencies and perils as might happen and grow by the wicked and dangerous practices of seditious sectaries [religious dissenters] and disloyal persons; be it enacted by the Queen's most excellent majesty, and [in] this present Parliament assembled . . . that if any person or persons above the age of sixteen years, which shall obstinately refuse to repair to some church, chapel, or usual place of common prayer, to hear divine service established by her majesty's laws . . . [or who] shall advisedly and maliciously move or persuade any other person whatsoever to forbear or abstain from coming to church to hear divine service, or to receive the communion according to her majesty's laws . . . shall be committed to prison, there to remain without bail . . . until they shall conform [to the rules stated in this act].

Quoted in Henry Gee and William John Hardy, eds., *Documents Illustrative of English Church History*. New York: Macmillan, 1896, pp. 492–98. http://history.hanover.edu/texts/ENGref/er86.html.

who were struggling to make ends meet, immigrating was an attractive way to obtain a fresh start in life. And for merchants and others of average or above-average means, the chance to grow rich beckoned. It became common knowledge that North America possessed abundant natural resources, including timber, furs, fish, tobacco, and precious metals. And both individuals and private companies were eager to exploit these valuable commodities. National governments, too, realized the potential of this new land, and they supported the colonies as a way to gain wealth, power, and influence on the international stage.

To ensure that England did not lose out on this potential economic bonanza, a group of English scholars and writers who became known as "mercantilists" tirelessly promoted colonization. The most influential was a preacher and scholar named Richard Hakluyt (1552–1616). Colonization would both enrich and glorify the mother country, he said, by supplying it with valuable goods from overseas and stimulating trade and new industries. Hakluyt wrote:

I marvel not a little that since the first discovery of America . . . after so [many] great conquests and plantings

The Hardworking Hakluyt

Richard Hakluyt (ca. 1552–1616) was a highly influential English writer and promoter of the exploration and settlement of North America. In his long career, he came to know most of his country's leading sea captains, explorers, and political figures, and he wrote several treatises about English voyages of discovery. While he worked hard to compile vast amounts of information for his writings, he found the effort worth it. In Principal Navigations, Voyages, Traffics, and Discoveries of the English Nation, *he wrote:*

What restless nights, what painful days, what heat, what cold I have endured; how many long and charge-able journeys I [have] traveled; how many famous libraries I have searched into; what variety of ancient and modern writers I have perused [read]; what a number of old records, patents, privileges, letters, etc., I have redeemed from obscurity and perishing. . . . [Yet] the honor and benefit of this [country] in which I live and breathe has made all difficulties seem easy, all pains and industry pleasant, and all expenses of light value [to] me.

Quoted in Edwin M. Bacon, ed., *English Voyages of Adventure and Discovery, Retold from Hakluyt.* New York: Scribner's 1908, p. 29.

[settlements] of the Spaniards and Portuguese there, that we of England could never have the grace to set foot in such fertile and temperate places as are left as yet [untaken by] them. Surely, if there were in us that desire to advance the honor of our country, which ought to be in every good man, we would not all this while have [hesitated to take possession] of those lands, which in [fairness] and right [we deserve].[24]

Involuntary Arrivals

One thing that the majority of early colonists—whether rich or poor—had in common was that they crossed the ocean of their own free will. However, a large minority of the population of most colonies, including England's, arrived involuntarily. Some were criminals, including convicted murderers. The government gave them a so-called choice—either be put to death in England by hanging or work as servants in the Americas for seven years. Up to twenty thousand convicts went to British America in the 1700s alone.

This kind of labor was called indentured servitude, and it was widespread. Convicts were not the only indentured servants. Because the cost of passage across the Atlantic was so high, poor folk often sold themselves into servitude for a set number of years in exchange for their fare. The deal was sealed by a written contract, many of which have survived. One for a London woman named Millicent How reads in part:

> Know all men that I, Millicent How of London, spinster [single woman] do firmly by [the present document] bind and oblige myself as a faithful and obedient servant in all things whatsoever, to serve and dwell with Capt. Joseph West, of the city of London, [and] merchant in the plantation, or province, of Carolina, according to laws and customs and orders for [indentured] servants . . . sealed this twentieth day of September, 1669.[25]

Worse still was the plight of black slaves bought by Europeans on Africa's western coasts and shipped in appallingly brutal conditions to the Americas. Between 1619 and 1776, some 350,000 African slaves were brought in chains to Britain's North American colonies. And in 1750, more than one-fifth of all the inhabitants of those colonies were slaves.

Female convicts arrive in Jamestown, Virginia, to serve as indentured servants.

An Indentured Servant Contract

A number of indentured servant contracts from colonial America have survived. Following is an except from one written in 1627 for an English iron worker named Richard Lowther, who sought to immigrate to the Jamestown Colony in Virginia.

This writing made the Last day of July/Anno Dom 1627 [is a contract] between Richard Lowther of Broome in [the] County of Bedford, [a] brewer . . . and Edward Hurd, citizen and iron monger of London. . . . Said Richard Lowther [has] hired himself and is become and by this [writing] does [agree to] bind himself to be remain and continue [in the service of] Edward Hurd, his heirs, and assigns to be by him or them sent and transported unto the country and land of Virginia, in the parts beyond the seas & to be by him or them employed upon his plantation there, for and during the space of four years to begin at the feast day of St. Michael Tharchangel . . . during which said term the said Richard Lowther shall and will truly employ and endeavor himself to the utmost of his power knowledge and skill to do and perform true and faithful service unto the said Edward Hurd, his heirs, and assigns in for and concerning all such labor and business as he or they shall think good to use and employ him the said Richard Lowther in, and [Lowther] shall and will be [an] obedient as a good and a faithful servant.

Quoted in "First Hand Accounts of Virginia, 1575–1705," Preston Davie Papers, Virginia Historical Society, Richmond. http://etext.lib.virginia.edu/etcbin/jamestown-browsemod?id=J1046.

One important difference between the black slaves and the white indentured servants was that the latter knew they would eventually be freed and have a chance at living a decent life. Another difference was that the white servants shared the same culture with the free settlers. They were all English (or else Scots, Dutch, or others who lived in the colonies under English dominion and laws). And they desired to remain that way. Hawke writes:

No one came eager to shed his English past. Whether they saw America as the land where failures got a second chance, an oasis where they could worship as they wished, or the place where a vanishing past could be preserved, all set out determined to remain what most of them were—Englishmen.[26]

This attitude was destined to endure for almost two centuries, until troubles between the colonists and their mother country brought about the watershed event known as the American Revolution.

Chapter Four

ESTABLISHMENT OF ROANOKE AND JAMESTOWN

Avid proponents of colonization like Richard Hakluyt had a strong influence on Queen Elizabeth I. Until her death in March 1603, she supported colonial ventures. For example, the queen awarded a grant to explorer Walter Raleigh, who was instrumental in the establishment of Roanoke, the first major English colony in North America. It was located off the coast of what is now North Carolina, a few miles south of Virginia's Chesapeake Bay region, which was destined to become one of the continent's major population centers. After Elizabeth's passing, her successor, James I, also showed an eagerness to support colonies. He granted a charter to the men who ended up founding the second English American colony, Jamestown, in the lower portion of the Chesapeake.

These expeditions were expensive, risky, and at first not very successful.

Roanoke was abandoned after only about three years, and both that colony and Jamestown experienced horrendous human suffering and high death tolls. One scholar writes:

> Between 1607 and 1624, four-fifths of the settlers at Jamestown died of disease, starvation, and Indian attacks. The winning of [an English] beachhead in Virginia cost far more casualties, in proportion to numbers engaged, than did the conquest of any of the Japanese-held islands in World War II.[27]

Yet that English beachhead was eventually won, despite the heavy costs. And the ultimate results were momentous. In time Jamestown became prosperous and in the decades that followed, other English settlers poured into the Chesapeake

Settlers arrive in the recently founded Jamestown colony, unaware of how many would soon die trying to colonize the land.

and mid-Atlantic region (as well as into New England, farther north). The creation of British America, which harbored the seeds of the future United States, had begun.

The Two Roanoke Expeditions

Roanoke is memorable not only because it was the first English colony in North America, but also because it very quickly progressed from an optimistic adventure, to a distressing tragedy, to an enduring mystery. Having acquired his grant from the queen, Walter Raleigh sent out more than a hundred settlers under the command of explorer Richard Grenville and experienced soldier Ralph Lane. They landed on Roanoke Island in August 1585.

Soon after arriving, Lane led several expeditions into nearby rivers and estuaries in hopes of establishing trade relations with local Indians. Such trade was essential to early colonists in both Roanoke and Jamestown because the ships that brought them to America were small and carried limited amounts of supplies and because the colonists were at first more interested in finding gold and other valuables than farming. Even if the settlers had begun farming right away, clearing land and growing enough crops to feed a colony could take a year or more, and in the mean time the settlers had to eat. Lane later wrote about one his side trips:

The [farthest we went] southward [was] Secotan being by estimation four score [80] miles distant from Roanoke. The passage [was] through a broad sound [yet] full of flats and shoals. We had but one boat with four oars [and] fifteen men with their furniture, baggage, and [enough food to last] seven days at the most.[28]

A map of the Roanoke area in the late 1500s, when English settlers arrived.

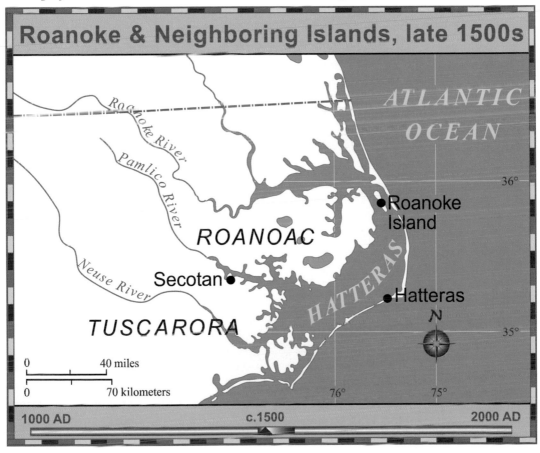

This first attempt to settle at Roanoke proved extremely difficult because of a chronic lack of food. Most of the Indians refused to trade after the settlers unwisely burned a native village (to punish a single Indian for supposedly stealing a drinking cup from the settlement). This unfortunate incident also led to periodic skirmishes between the whites and Indians. The colonists thought about abandoning the settlement. And when, after a trip to the Caribbean, English mariner Francis Drake visited Roanoke in June 1586, they accepted his offer to take them back to England.

In July 1587, a second group of colonists, also numbering more than a hundred, arrived on the island under the command of John White. Among them was his daughter, Eleanor, who was pregnant. On August 18 she gave birth to the first English child born in the Americas, named Virginia Dare.

Meanwhile, finding sufficient food proved no less a problem than it had been for the earlier colonists. So later that year White returned to England, promising to return soon with large stores of supplies. However, after reaching the mother country, White had serious difficulties finding a suitable ship for the trip back to Roanoke. At the time, the English were being threatened by a huge enemy war fleet, the famous Spanish Armada, and all reliable vessels were pressed into military service.

An Eerie Silence

As a result of these delays, White was unable to get back to Roanoke until August 1590. To his surprise and dread, instead of a bustling town he found an empty campsite enveloped in an eerie silence. Even the houses, made of wood and thatch, were gone. He later recalled:

> At my departure from them in Anno [the year] 1587, I willed them that if they should happen to be distressed, [they] should carve [a Maltese cross on a tree or post], but we found no such sign of distress. And having well considered of this, we passed toward the place where they were left in sundry [assorted] houses, but we found the houses taken down, [and various artifacts] thrown here and there, almost overgrown with grass and weeds. [We also] found five chests, that had been carefully hidden [and] three were my own, and about the place many of my things spoiled and broken.[29]

Although White and his men found no carved cross, they did find two carvings left by the settlers. One consisted of the letters "CRO," etched into a tree trunk near the beach. The other was the word *Croatoan*, carved on one of the posts in the settlement's stockade, which was still standing. From this evidence, White speculated that the colonists may have gone to live with the friendly Indians who inhabited nearby Croatoan

When John White returned to Roanoke he found the colony empty and the word "Croatoan" carved into one of the stockade posts, implying the settlers may have fled to Croatoan Island.

Island (now Hatteras Island). He wanted to go to Croatoan and investigate. But the sailors he was with were afraid they too might disappear, and they insisted on leaving immediately. As a result, the lost colonists were never found.

Over the years, there have been a number of theories about what happened to the Roanoke settlers. One is that most or all of them starved to death. They were already in dire need of supplies, and some researchers think that a severe drought may have struck in 1588 and pushed them over the edge. Other theories suggest that hostile Indians killed the colonists; that a force of Span-ish soldiers, seeing Roanoke as competi-tion for their own New World colonies, killed them; that a powerful hurricane wiped out the settlement; and that the settlers intermarried with friendly Indi-ans and lived out their lives with them.

However Roanoke met its end, in ret-rospect it is easy to discern some of the reasons it failed. First, instead of land-ing at a site favorable for navigation, the colonists chose a location hard for ships to reach. Also, the Roanoke area was swampy and hard to farm. In truth, there had been little concern for finding fertile land and growing crops, as the main goals were to find gold and other

Modern Descendants of the Roanoke Settlers?

Of the several existing theories for what happened to the settlers of Roanoke Colony, one of the more controversial maintains that they intermarried with local Indians. Author Josh Clark writes:

[O]ne] widely held theory of what became of the Roanoke colonists: They assimilated into some friendly Native American tribe. Over the course of generations, intermarriage between the natives and the English would produce a third, distinct group. This group may be the Lumbee tribe. The Lumbee tribe is native to North Carolina, yet no certain lineage can be pinned down. The tribe's oral history links them to the Roanoke settlers, and this tradition is supported by some of their surnames and the tribe's ability to read and write English. Family names of some of the Roanoke colonists, like Dial, Hyatt and Taylor, were shared by Lumbee tribe members as early as 1719. The settlers who met them were astonished to find Native Americans that had gray eyes and spoke English. [However, a number of scholars dispute this story, and] even within the Lumbee tribe, the veracity [truth] of the group's link to the Roanoke colonists is in dispute.

Josh Clark, "What Happened to the Lost Colony of Roanoke?" HowStuffWorks, http://history.howstuffworks.com/american-history/roanoke-colony2.htm.

riches rumored to exist in the mysterious North American wilderness. "Roanoke demonstrated that the distracting pursuit of immediate wealth worked against the laborious and patient development of a plantation colony," historian Alan Taylor points out. He also writes:

Why cultivate corn when an overland exploration might yield a gold mine, or sea raiding might capture Spanish bullion [gold]? Eager to search for Spanish ships, the English mariners dumped colonists and their supplies with an indecent, wasteful haste, [and] the poor location reinforced their aversion, for mariners dreaded the shoal waters and adverse winds as a graveyard for ships and sailors.[30]

Early Jamestown

The English tried to correct some of these mistakes in their next colonization effort at Jamestown two decades later. Chesapeake Bay and its adjoining estuaries were considerably more navigable than the waters off Roanoke. The Chesapeake region was also very fertile and its estuaries and rivers were rich in fish, shellfish, edible plants, and small game.

The Jamestown venture began in earnest with King James's grant of a charter to the newly formed Virginia Company of London in April 1606. The company was headed by three partners—explorer Bartholomew Gosnold; a member of Parliament, Edward Wingfield; and soldier John Smith. These men obtained financial backing from London merchants and others to establish a colony in the Chesapeake Bay area.

In December of that year, 120 colonists departed England in three ships, the *Susan Constant*, *Godspeed*, and *Discovery*, bound for Virginia. And on May 14, 1607, the expedition landed on Jamestown Island, on the banks of the James River, 60 miles (97km) from the mouth of Chesapeake Bay. One reason for choosing this site was that it was easily defendable against Spanish or French raiders who might try to attack the new colony. Although they avoided many of the mistakes made by the Roanoke settlers, the new colonists repeated one. Namely, much of Jamestown Island was composed of low-lying, swampy terrain. One of the colony's early governors, Thomas Gates, explains:

Jamestown [is] seated in somewhat an unwholesome and sickly air, by reason it is in a marsh ground, low, flat to the river, and has no fresh water springs serving the town, [except] what we draw from a well six or seven fathoms [about 42 feet/13m] deep, fed by the brackish river oozing into it, from [where] I [truly] believe, [have caused] many diseases and sicknesses [among] our people.[31]

The Jamestown colony built a tall stockade fence to protect against possible Indian attacks.

In spite of the less-than-ideal location, the settlers forged ahead and erected a fortified trading post, several timber and thatch houses, a church, and a large storehouse. They also built a tall stockade fence for protection against possible Indian attacks. As the months rolled by, it looked as if the colony would prosper. John Smith explored the surrounding area and established trade relations with a couple of local Indian tribes, among them the Nansemond. In October 1608 a second group of settlers arrived with food and supplies. In addition to a number of Englishmen, they included several German and Polish craftsmen and a Swiss mineral prospector.

The Starving Time

These hopeful beginnings were soon overshadowed by misfortune. One problem was the onset of a severe drought. Another was that a strong local Indian leader, Powhatan, who was leery of the colonists and their motives, significantly cut back on trade of food items. Finally the settlers themselves became their own worst enemies by failing to grow enough of their own food. According to Taylor:

Even when healthy, many colonists refused to work diligently at raising corn to feed themselves. They were an unstable [mix] of gentlemen-adventurers in command and poor vagrants rounded up from the streets of London and forcibly sent to Virginia. Neither group had much prior experience with work. In England, birth and wealth had screened the gentlemen from manual labor, while the

A Song to See Them Off

To commemorate the colonists' departure for Virginia in 1607, Englishman Michael Drayton composed a ballad that was sung on the docks as the ships left. Two of the verses read:

And cheerful at sea,
Success you still entice,
To get the pearl and gold,
And Ours to hold,

Virginia!
Earth's only paradise.
Where nature has in store,
Fowl, venison, and fish,
And the fruitful soil,
Without your toil,
Three harvests more,
All greater than you wish.

Quoted in John C. Metcalf, *American Literature*. Richmond, VA: Johnson, 1914, p. 14.

A Miserable First Winter

The settlers of Jamestown Colony endured a miserable first winter (1607–1608). Colonist George Percy describes some of the suffering:

Our men were destroyed with cruel diseases, as swellings, [and fevers]. Some departed [died] suddenly, but for the most part they died of mere famine. There were never Englishmen left in a foreign country in such misery as we were in this new discovered Virginia. . . . Our food was but a small can of barley sod in water, to five men a day, our drink cold water taken out of the river, which was at a flood very salty, [and] at low tide full of slime and filth, which was the destruction of many of our men. Thus we lived for the space of five months in this miserable distress, not having five able men to [guard us]. If it had not pleased God to have put a terror in the savages' hearts, we [would] have all perished.

Quoted in Lyon Tyler, ed., *Narratives of Early Virginia, 1606–1625.* New York: Barnes and Noble, 1946, p. 21.

vagrants, for want of employment, had learned to survive by begging and stealing.[32]

The combination of these factors caused a terrible famine in the colony during the winter of 1609–1610, which the settlers later came to call the "starving time." Of the roughly 214 colonists in residence at the start of the winter, fewer than a hundred were still alive in the spring. These bedraggled survivors decided to abandon the colony and go back to England. But at the last minute a relief expedition commanded by Thomas West (later called "Lord Delaware") arrived with plenty of food, along with new settlers, including a doctor.

Forging a New World

After that, the colony's fortunes began to turn around, slowly at first but then by leaps and bounds. One of the settlers, John Rolfe, tried his hand at growing tobacco, a crop no one else was willing to raise. By 1612 he was collecting a comfortable profit by selling the tobacco in England, at which point other colonists decided to follow his lead. Within a few years Jamestown could not keep up with demand for the crop in the mother country. The colony "went tobacco-mad," according to historian Samuel E. Morison. "It was even grown in the streets," and "as early as 1618 Virginia exported 50,000 pounds' weight of tobacco to England."[33]

The following year (1619) proved important for the now-thriving Jamestown.

Farm workers harvest tobacco leaves on a Virginia plantation in 1612. Tobacco quickly became the most profitable crop in America.

First, the leading colonists formed the first representative, or democratic, legislature in North America—the House of Burgesses (which was to play a crucial role later, in the prelude to the American Revolution). Second, the first single women the colony had seen, ninety of them, arrived to provide wives for the many single male settlers. Third, the first black African slaves in British America arrived. (Historians have long known about twenty blacks who came in August. But recent research suggests that thirty-two others may have arrived a few months earlier.)

Over time, many other towns were established in Virginia, which became a crown, or government-controlled, colony in 1624. Jamestown remained the capital of the colony until 1698, when the seat of government moved to nearby Williamsburg. Thereafter, Jamestown steadily faded in importance, and its residents moved away to other towns. As its buildings rapidly decayed, Jamestown was eventually absorbed into a few large local farms.

Although Jamestown is gone, its history and impact remain. The Jamestown settlers established "lines of development that have continued to influence American society ever since," notes scholar James Horn. "At Jamestown, the peoples of America, Europe, and Africa first encountered one another, lived and worked alongside each other," and "together they shaped a new world and forged a new people."[34]

Chapter Five

FOUNDING PLYMOUTH AND MASSACHUSETTS BAY

Bartholomew Gosnold and John Smith are among the few individuals in the early stages of English colonization who had an impact on settlement in both the mid-Atlantic region and New England. Both men were partners in the Virginia Company of London, which established Jamestown. But a few years before that company formed, Gosnold had explored the coasts of Massachusetts. And the accounts of his voyage caused numerous people in England to consider settling in that region.

Gosnold's discoveries and the interest they sparked also set in motion the creation of reliable maps of New England coasts. In 1605 and 1606 French explorer Samuel de Champlain mapped the coast of Massachusetts and made note of a number of areas that he deemed suitable for colonization. They included Gloucester, situated north of what is now Boston; Plymouth, lying south of Boston; and Eastham and Chatham on Cape Cod. Maps of the Massachusetts Bay region were also drawn by Dutch explorers Adrian Block and Henrik Christiansen in 1614.

As for Smith's contributions, he explored the coasts north of Cape Cod in 1614 and coined the term *New England* for the general region. Also, his use of the word *Massachusetts* (after the local Massachusett Indian people) to describe the Massachusetts Bay area became universally accepted. After returning to England, Smith published the book *A Description of New England*. In it he provides a detailed overview of the terrain, harbors, flora and fauna, and native peoples of the region. He wrote:

I have seen at least 40 several habitations upon the sea coast, [and] about 25 excellent good harbors. In many there is anchorage for 500 . . . ships of any burden [weight]. . . . And [I saw] more than 200 islands overgrown with good timber. . . . The country of Massachusetts [is] the paradise of all those parts, for here are many islands all planted with corn, groves, mulberries, [and] salvage gardens. . . . The coast is for the most part high, clay, sandy cliffs. The sea coast as you pass [displays] large corn fields and great troupes [groups] of well-proportioned people [Indians].[35]

Journeys of the Separatists

Together the accounts of Gosnold's voyage and Smith's book about coastal New England encouraged the first major wave of colonization in Massachusetts. The initial settlers in the region, the Separatists and Puritans, saw moving to North America as a way to escape religious persecution. Both groups grew out of opposition to the Church of England. But the Puritans tried to change the church from within, while others chose to separate completely from the church and thereby became known as Separatists.

At this time opposition to the church was a crime. So at first the Separatists

French explorer Samuel de Champlain created many maps that became useful tools for other explorers of North America.

The Separatists, later known as Pilgrims, left England on the Mayflower *on September 16, 1620.*

worshipped in secret. Eventually, however, some were discovered, harassed, and threatened with prosecution. So in 1608 they fled to Holland, which allowed freedom of religion. The authorities in the Dutch city of Leyden declared, "[We] refuse no honest persons free ingress to come and have their residence in this city, provided that such persons behave themselves and submit to the laws and ordinances."[36]

The Separatists did not stay long in Holland, however. In part, this was because they came to fear that Dutch culture, which was much more progressive than their own ultraconservative customs, might corrupt them, especially their children. One of the group's lead-

ers, William Bradford, later wrote that some of the children were affected by "the great licentiousness [immorality] of youth in that country, and the manifold [many] temptations of the place, [and so we] saw [they] would be in danger to degenerate and to be corrupted."[37]

After long discussions about where to go, the Separatists decided to try to start a new life in North America. They obtained permission from King James I on the condition that their religious beliefs would receive no official recognition from the government. Their small ship, the *Mayflower*, departed on September 16, 1620.

A Harsh Winter

The passengers of the *Mayflower* did not refer to themselves as Pilgrims, a term for them that did not come into general use until the early 1800s. However, most modern histories of the Separatists call them Pilgrims upon their arrival in New England in November 1620. The first land the Pilgrims sighted was Cape Cod. They anchored the ship in the harbor of what is now Provincetown, at the tip of the cape, and for the next few weeks the group's leaders explored the nearby coasts in hopes of finding a favorable place to settle. On December 21, 1620, these men came ashore at what is now Plymouth and liked what they saw. One later recalled:

> On Monday we sounded the harbor [measured the water for depth], and found it a very good harbor for

our shipping. We marched also into the land and found diverse cornfields and little running brooks, a place very good for [settling], so we returned to our ship again with good news to the rest of our people, which did much comfort their hearts.[38]

One thing that soon discomforted the Pilgrims' hearts was the harshness of the ongoing winter. In addition to the bitter cold, there was a shortage of food, and by the end of December six people were dead. More died in the months that fol-lowed and in late March 1621 Bradford wrote:

> This month, thirteen of our number die. There die sometimes two or three a day. Of one hundred persons, scarce fifty remain. The living [are] scarce able to bury the dead. The well [are] not sufficient to tend the sick.[39]

Prosperity and Growth

The spring brought reasons for hope, however. Over the course of some weeks,

The Trials of Plymouth Rock

Each year many people visit Plymouth, Massachusetts, in part to see the famous Plymouth Rock, the traditional site of the Pilgrims' first landing. According to scholar George F. Willison, however, that rock did not achieve any particular distinction until long after the Pilgrims were in their graves. In his book Saints and Strangers, *Willison writes:*

For a century and a half after the landing . . . the rock lay unmarked, almost unnoticed. Until 1769, on the eve of [American] independence, it was just another gray granite boulder, one more troublesome bit of glacial debris littering a white arc of beach. . . . For another century, it was dragged, a broken and mutilated fragment, up and down the streets of Plymouth—first to Town Square, to make a revolutionary holiday; then to Pilgrim Hall, as a museum piece. . . . Restored at length to the beach and enshrined [inside] an elaborate Victorian stone canopy, the rock enjoyed a half century of comparative quiet and repose before it was snatched up again [and] dumped where it has since remained, at tidewater, sheltered and quite overshadowed by a lustrous Grecian temple of Quincy granite.

George F. Willison, *Saints and Strangers*, New York: Time, 1945, pp. 1–2.

Plymouth Colony flourished due to the colonists' hard work and the help of the Indians. In 1621 the Pilgrims celebrated the first Thanksgiving with the Indians.

the settlers saw Indians moving about nearby, and some Pilgrims worried there might be an attack. But their fears were put to rest when one of the natives walked into the colony and welcomed them in perfect English. His name was Samoset, and he had learned English from some English fishermen in Maine. The colonists soon met other Indians, including Squanto, who also spoke English (having spent several years in England). The friendly Squanto showed the Pilgrims the best places to fish and taught them how to grow corn.

Partly because of the Indians' help and partly because of the colonists' own hard work, the colony began to prosper. And in the autumn of 1621 the Pilgrims held a big feast to offer thanksgiving to God (which became the precedent for the modern Thanksgiving holiday). Bradford, now governor of the colony, invited a number of Indians, and all in attendance stuffed themselves with wild turkey, duck, goose, deer, fish, and corn.

As the years progressed, Plymouth continued to thrive. Other English Separatists, along with many non-Separatists, arrived

A Slice of Native Life

While searching along the shores of Massachusetts Bay for a suitable site to build a settlement, the Separatists (later called the Pilgrims) found some recently abandoned native houses. Following is the recollection of the discovery by one settler, whose identity is unknown.

The houses were made with long young sapling trees, bended and both ends stuck into the ground. . . . The door was not over a yard high [and] made of a mat to open. The chimney was a wide open hole in the top, for which they had a mat to cover [it] when they pleased. . . . In the midst of [the houses] were four little trunches [stakes] knocked into the ground, and small sticks laid over, on which they hung their pots and what they had to [cook]. Round about the fire they laid on mats, which are their beds. . . . In the houses we found wooden bowls, trays, and dishes, earthen pots, [and] handbaskets made of crabshells wrought together.

Quoted in Anonymous, *A Relation or Journal of the Proceedings of the Plantation Settled at Plymouth in New England*, in *Mourt's Relation: A Journal of the Pilgrims at Plymouth*, ed. Dwight B. Heath. Carlisle, MA: Applewood, 1963, pp. 47–48.

and the colony became so crowded that some of the Pilgrims left and established new towns in the area. "There was no longer any holding them together," Bradford writes, "but now they must of necessity go [their separate ways]. They were scattered all over the [Massachusetts] Bay [region]."[40] By 1640, the Plymouth Colony consisted of eight towns with an overall population of some twenty-five hundred people.

Hard Working, Educated, and Intolerant

Back in England, meanwhile, the Puritans, who were still unhappy about the Anglican Church, heard about the success of the Separatists in North America and decided to establish a colony of their own. In 1628 a group of about fifty Puritans founded a town at Salem, about 50 miles (80km) north of Plymouth. Their task was to build houses and plant crops in preparation for the main force of Puritans who would follow in two years time.

According to the plan, more than a thousand Puritans arrived in 1630 under the leadership of John Winthrop. But as one of the new arrivals, Thomas Dudley, later recalled, "Salem, where we landed, pleased us not. And for that purpose some [men] were sent to the Bay to search up the rivers for a convenient place."[41] That place turned out to be Boston (about 15 miles/24km south of Salem), established on September 17, 1630, on a peninsula surrounded on three sides by water. The newcomers also founded some smaller towns in the area, including Dorchester, Watertown, and Medford.

In the ten years that followed, thousands of other Puritans arrived in Massachusetts. Most settled in Boston, but some set up new towns in the immediate area, among them Concord, Charlestown, and Weymouth. Unlike Roanoke, Jamestown, and Plymouth, the Massachusetts Bay Colony prospered almost from the beginning. This was partly because the expeditions that brought settlers to the new colony were very well planned and organized. John C. Miller, a professor of American history, writes:

> Instead of wasting time looking for nonexistent gold or a passage to the [East Indies], the Puritans immediately got down to the business of clearing land, building houses, and planting crops. Nor did John Winthrop and other Puritan leaders, even though they possessed the rank of "gentlemen," disdain to work with their hands.[42]

Puritan expeditions were successful because the colonies were well planned and the Puritans worked hard, building houses and planting crops.

Many of the new colonists who settled in Boston and the surrounding towns were children. They benefited from the fact that the Puritans were big believers in education for both genders (in large part because they felt that a certain level of learning was necessary for proper study of the Bible). True to this principle, they established the Boston Latin School in 1635. It was the first public school in North America. The Puritans also founded the continent's first college—Harvard University—between 1636 and 1638.

A less admirable aspect of Puritan life (by today's standards) was a series of extremely strict rules and laws. These grew out of the group's religious conservatism and intolerance for any ideas or views they disagreed with. A person who differed with the group's leaders, especially in religious matters, was seen as a criminal. A colonist who missed attending church was whipped or else forced to sit all day in the stocks, a wooden contraption that kept one's hands and feet locked in one position. One dissenter, Salem resident Roger Williams, argued that people should be allowed to worship in whatever manner they wanted. Seeing him as an evildoer, the authorities exiled him in 1635. Soon afterward Williams established a new colony, with more tolerant rules, in nearby Rhode Island.

The Puritans' austere rules and laws also extended into their personal lives, in which nearly every form of play and recreation was forbidden. "Puritan lawmakers compiled a seemingly exhaustive list of prohibited 'carnal delights,'" Miller writes:

> such as attending plays, dancing around a Maypole, bowling on the green, playing at shuffleboard, quoits [in which players toss rings onto an upright stake], dice, and cards. [And] a French dancing master was ordered out of town lest "profane and promiscuous dancing" corrupt the morals of the citizens.[43]

The Puritans and Pilgrims Unite

As much as the Puritan colonists disliked and distrusted outside influences, they were increasingly forced to interact with the peoples who lived alongside them. Among them were the Native Americans who had inhabited the region before the Europeans' arrival. Some Puritans wanted to befriend the Indians and convert them to Christianity. As part of this effort, colonist John Eliot set up some special villages for the converts, known as "praying Indians." The first was at Natick, several miles west of Boston. In contrast, other colonists considered Indians to be inferior and in the way of white settlement. So they stole tribal lands and cheated Indians when trading with them, provoking wars.

Fortunately for the Puritans, the other close neighbors they had to deal with—the Pilgrims of Plymouth—were culturally much more like themselves.

Puritans had strict laws and colonists who missed church ended up in the stocks all day.

Plymouth and Massachusetts Bay competed for land, resources, and markets for decades. But the fact that the residents of both colonies were English (or of some other European extraction) and Christians with similar beliefs made their union seem inevitable. That pivotal event occurred in 1691. England's reigning monarchs, William III and Mary II, merged Plymouth with Massachusetts Bay, thereby creating the Massachusetts Colony, with its capital at Boston.

The new colony grew rapidly. By 1765, its population soared past 250,000, of which about a tenth lived in Boston, then the largest city in British America. At the time, at least 80 percent of the colony's residents were English; most of the rest were Scots, Irish, French, and Germans. Yet nearly all swiftly came to

An Early Colonial Poet

The Puritans not only emphasized learning, but also recognized the importance of educating women along with men. One of these women was Anne Bradstreet, a resident of Massachusetts Bay Colony and the first woman in the Americas to have her writings published. Among her surviving poems is the following ode titled, "To My Dear and Loving Husband."

If ever two were one, then surely we.
If ever man were loved by wife, then thee.
If ever wife was happy in a man,
Compare with me, ye women, if you can.
I prize thy love more than whole Mines of gold
Or all the riches that the East doth hold.
My love is such that Rivers cannot quench,
Nor ought but love from thee give recompense.
Thy love is such I can no way repay.
The heavens reward thee manifold, I pray.
Then while we live, in love let's so persevere
That when we live no more, we may live ever.

Quoted in John Harvard Ellis, ed, *The Works of Anne Bradstreet in Prose and Verse.* Charlestown, SC: Cutter, 1867. Early Americas Digital Archive, www.mith2.umd.edu/eada/html/display.php?docs=bradstreet_tomydear.xml&action=show.

think of themselves not as Europeans living abroad, but rather as New Englanders and Americans. Historian Samuel E. Morison explains:

Other European colonists in America regarded themselves as Frenchmen, Englishmen, Dutchmen, or Spaniards living in America, and looked forward to returning "home." Not so the New Englanders. The first person on record to use the word *American* for a European colonist rather than an Indian was Puritan Cotton Mather in 1684. The "Yankees," as they were called in the next century, regarded America as their home.[44]

This natural feeling of separateness from "mother Europe" was destined to have momentous consequences later.

Chapter Six

THE MID-ATLANTIC AND SOUTHERN COLONIES

I n the decades following the establishment of the Virginia and Massachusetts colonies, British America, centered on North America's eastern seaboard, grew rapidly. New colonies were founded, their lands eventually stretching from New Hampshire in the north to Georgia in the south. And the region's overall population increased from about 2,000 in 1625 to 200,000 in 1688 to 434,000 in 1715.

The Dutch and New York

One of the fastest growing and economically prosperous of these new colonies was New York, which began as a small Dutch settlement. After Giovanni da Verrazano explored what is now New York Harbor and Long Island in the 1520s, the next significant exploration of the area was conducted by English sea captain Henry Hudson. In 1609 under contract with the Dutch, he surveyed coastal New York and then sailed up the river that now bears his name. After returning to the Netherlands, he reported that the region was both hospitable and rich in furs and other natural resources.

Based on Hudson's findings, the Dutch financed more expeditions to the area, which became known as New Netherland. The first settlement they established was a trading post called Fort Nassau (later Fort Orange), on the Hudson River near present-day Albany, in 1614. For several years it had only fifty or so residents, mostly fur traders who exchanged goods with the Indians living along the Hudson.

Later, in 1625, the Dutch established the town of New Amsterdam (later New York City), on Manhattan Island. The

A map of New Netherland, a successful colony settled by the Dutch in the early 1600s.

ple [to the colony], received a feudal domain [huge estate] on the Hudson, with a fifteen-mile river front, exclusive fishing and hunting privileges, civil and criminal [authority], and the right to share the fur trade with the [colony's backers].[45]

With this new arrangement, New Netherland's leaders encouraged settlement on Manhattan, on neighboring Long Island, and along the shores of the Hudson. The population quickly grew. Although it was a Dutch-run colony, its demographic and cultural makeup was not strictly Dutch. Rather it featured a diverse mix of Dutch, Swedish, German, French, black African, and Native American languages and customs. As a result, there was a good deal of religious tolerance and promotion of liberal ideas and social harmony that were retained in later generations (and still exist there today).

Seized by the English

The transformation from Dutch New Netherland to English New York occurred as the result of increasing friction between the Dutch colonists and the English settlers who lived to the northeast. At first, the two groups had minimal contact. But as the years went by, English colonists increasingly settled in what is now southern Connecticut, an area then claimed by New Netherland. The Dutch protested. But their population and military resources were far smaller than those of the English colonies, which took full

following year, in what became one of the most famous land deals in history, they bought the island from some local Indians for the modern equivalent of about a thousand dollars.

New Amsterdam possessed a fine harbor and a strategic location between Virginia and the New England colonies. So in 1629 the Dutch began encouraging farmers and other permanent residents to settle in the colony. Spearheading this effort were men known as patroons. Historian Samuel E. Morison explains:

A patroon was a person who, in return for bringing about fifty peo-

The Short-Lived New Sweden

Among the many European nations that desired to achieve footholds in North America in the 1600s was Sweden. In 1637 a group of Swedish, Dutch, and German businessmen got together and established the New Sweden Company. Its main goal was to engage in the then lucrative trade in North American furs and tobacco. Late that same year, settlers in two ships, the *Kalmar Nyckel* and *Fogel Grip*, left Sweden and in March 1638 landed at Delaware Bay. The colonists proceeded to erect a fortification, which they named Fort Christina, in honor of Sweden's twelve-year-old queen.

In the seventeen years that followed, twelve more Swedish expeditions brought settlers to the colony, known as New Sweden. In those years the colony thrived and even expanded, as settlers built farms and houses on both sides of the Delaware River. But eventually the Dutch in nearby New Netherland intervened. In 1654 seven Dutch warships appeared and demanded that the Swedes surrender,

which they did. Although no more Swedish colonies were established in America thereafter, many Swedes later immigrated to colonial British America and later the United States.

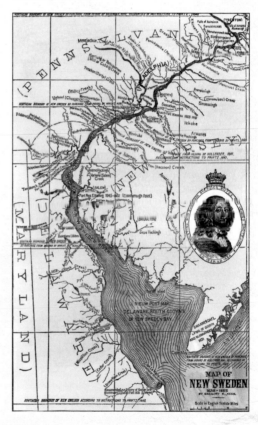

A map of New Sweden, near the Delaware Bay.

advantage of New Netherland's weak defense of its frontier.

Many people on both sides realized that it was only a matter of time before the English made a more openly aggressive move against the Dutch settlements. And sure enough, in March 1664 England's king Charles II decided to annex New Netherland. The takeover began on August 27 of that year. Four English warships entered New Amsterdam's harbor and demanded that the Dutch surrender. Seeing no other choice, the governor of New Netherland complied and the transfer of power occurred without the firing of a shot.

The surrender terms were very generous and moderate. One of them reads, "All people shall still continue free denizens and enjoy their lands, houses, goods, ships, wherever they are within this country, and dispose of them as they please."[46] Most of the other terms are similar in tone. Such reasonableness helped to ensure that the tolerant attitudes and liberal atmosphere that already existed in the colony would continue. Once the surrender was complete, New Netherland became New York. And the following year New Amsterdam was renamed New York City.

The Founding of Maryland

Lying not far south of New York was another important mid-Atlantic colony, Maryland, which began as a haven for England's persecuted Catholics. The wealthy and influential George Calvert, the first Lord Baltimore, himself an Irish Catholic, applied to King Charles I for a royal charter to set up the colony. The crown granted the charter in 1632.

The first expedition mounted by Calvert, consisting of about two hundred settlers in two ships, the *Ark* and

A Dutch town on Manhattan Island in the 1600s. The small military resources of the Dutch were no match for those of the English, who took over New Netherland in 1664.

The success of the Maryland colony was largely due to the generosity of Indians, who supplied the colony with food, such as the maize being harvested here.

the *Dove*, landed in Maryland in March 1634. From the start, many of the colonists were Protestants. However, those in authority were all Catholics. This mix of faiths ensured that religious tolerance would be recognized in the colony's laws and rigorously upheld in everyday life.

In the years that followed, the region lured many more people, in part because of its appealing climate and fertile soil. In his 1666 book about Maryland, English author George Alsop wrote:

[Maryland is] extraordinarily pleasant and fertile. Pleasant, in respect of the multitude of navigable rivers and creeks that conveniently and most profitably lodge within the arms of her green, spreading, and delightful woods; whose natural womb (by her plenty) maintains and preserves the several diversities of animals that . . . inhabit her woods; as she does otherwise generously [enhance] this piece of Earth with almost all sorts of vegetables, as well as flowers with their varieties of colors and smells.[47]

The original Maryland Colony was considerably larger than present-day Maryland, which is one of the smallest

Tobacco Cultivation in Maryland

The seventeenth-century English writer George Alsop wrote extensively about Maryland. In the following excerpt, he tells how the Indians first cultivated tobacco, after which it became a major crop of the colonists.

Tobacco is the only solid staple commodity of this province. The use of it was first found out by the Indians, many ages ago, and transferred into Christendom by that great discoverer of America Columbus. It's generally made by all the inhabitants of this province, and between the months of March and April they sow the seed (which is much smaller then mustard-seed) in small beds and patches dug up and . . . about May the plants commonly appear green in those beds. In June they are transplanted from their beds, and set in little hillocks in distant rows, dug up for the same purpose; some twice or thrice they are weeded, and succored from their illegitimate leaves that would be peeping out from the body of the stalk. . . . About the middle of September they cut the tobacco down, and carry it into houses, (made for that purpose) to bring it to its purity. And after it has attained, by a convenient attendance upon time, to its perfection, it is then tied up in bundles, and packed into hogs-heads, and then laid by [stored] for the trade.

George Alsop, *A Character of the Province of Maryland*, ed. Newton D. Mereness. Cleveland, OH: Burrows, 1902. Early Americas Digital Archive, www.mith2 .umd.edu/eada/html/display.php?docs=alsop_character .xml&action=show.

states in the Union. Calvert's charter granted the colonists all the lands lying between New York and Virginia, including territories lying far inland. Later, Maryland lost much of this inland land to Pennsylvania (and some was used to create the District of Columbia after the American Revolution).

Maryland's economy prospered throughout most of the colonial period. At first, the colonists owed much of this success to the generosity and hospitality of the local Indians. They supplied the colony with food and even allowed its residents to use native huts as their first churches. One colonist later recalled:

Daily the [Indians] are here in our houses and [are] content to be with us, bringing sometimes turkeys, sometimes squirrels as big as English rabbits. . . . At other times [they bring] fine white cakes, partridges, oysters ready boiled and stewed, and do [display a] smiling countenance when they see us and will fish and hunt for us [and] all this [while uttering] very few words, but we have [learned to gather] their meaning by signs [hand gestures].[48]

Later, Maryland's economy, like that of Virginia, became heavily dependent on raising tobacco for sale to European markets. That crop became so plentiful in Maryland that it was sometimes used as local currency. And farmers were so preoccupied with growing it that the colonial government eventually had to pass a law requiring them to grow corn, too, to ensure food for the colony. In order to make large profits from tobacco, farmers needed cheap labor. So Maryland growers steadily came to use many indentured servants and black slaves. By 1755 a hefty 40 percent of the colony's inhabitants were black. This approach paid off. Throughout the 1700s the colonial capital, Baltimore, was the second most important port in the southern English colonies (after Charleston, South Carolina).

Pennsylvania's Welcoming Atmosphere

Just as Massachusetts became a refuge for Puritans and Maryland for Catholics, English Quakers created a sanctuary in Pennsylvania. The new colony was named for its benefactor, William Penn, the son of an English admiral. The younger Penn converted to the Quaker faith, then seen by most English as radical and antisocial, at the age of twenty-two, and his father was so upset that he threw his son out of the house. The penniless young man went to live with fellow Quakers, but later reconciled with his father.

When the elder Penn died in 1670, the king owed him sixteen thousand pounds. To settle this debt, the crown gave William Penn 45,000 square miles (116,549sq. km) of land lying west of the Delaware River. At the time, this made him the world's largest landowner. The deal was that Penn would encourage Quakers to leave England and settle in his new colony. From the start, however, Penn was determined to promote religious freedom and allow anyone, including Native Americans, to live together in peace and harmony. While the colony drew large numbers of Quakers, it also attracted non-Quakers from England, Germany, the Netherlands, and elsewhere.

Nearly all of these settlers were hard working and/or skilled in business or crafts. So the colony swiftly became one of the most financially successful of all the English North American colonies. According to historian Alan Taylor, many of the more skilled incoming colonists

lingered in Philadelphia as artisans and merchants. The merchants tended to be "weighty Friends" with sound credit, sober reputations, and extensive trade contacts throughout the [British] empire. Their shared faith endowed the far-flung Quaker merchants with a mutual trust that afforded a critical advantage in the competitive conduct of long-distance commerce. [As a result] Philadelphia's merchant community became the wealthiest in the colonies.[49]

Another reason that Pennsylvania prospered during the colonial period was that its live-and-let-live policy toward Native Americans ensured a prolonged period of peace and security. Unlike settlers in several other colonies, Penn and his associates acknowledged that the Indians owned the land before the Europeans arrived. And they treated the local natives with respect. "I would have you well observe that I am very sensible of the unkindness and injustice that has been too much exercised toward you," Penn told local Indian leaders. "I have great love and regard toward you and desire to win and gain your love and friendship by a kind, just, and peaceful life."[50] True to his word, Penn required settlers to buy land from the natives before inhabiting it. As a result, the Indians prospered, too, and this welcoming atmosphere inspired Native Americans

William Penn and the Quakers were friendly toward Native Americans and supported their religious freedom.

The Abundant Carolina Woods

One of the early English settlers in Carolina, Robert Horne, wrote about the region's abundant forests and other natural resources, saying in part:

The land is of diverse sorts as in all countries of the world. That which lies near the sea is sandy and barren, but bears many tall trees, which make good timber for several uses; and this sandy ground is by experienced men thought to be one cause of the healthfulness of the place. But up the river about 20 or 30 miles, where they have made a town, called Charles Town, there is plenty of as rich ground as any in the world. It is a blackish mold upon a red sand, and under that a clay, but in some places is rich ground of a grayer color . . . which proves very good; and lime they have also for building. The whole country consists of stately woods, groves, marshes and meadows; it abounds with variety of as brave oaks as [your] eye can behold, great bodies tall and straight from 60 to 80 foot [high]. In the barren sandy ground grow most stately pines, white and red cedars, ash, birch, holly, chestnut and walnut-trees of great growth and very plentiful. There are [also] many sorts of fruit trees, [including] peach, wild cherries, [and] mulberry. . . . The woods are stored with deer and wild turkeys, of a great magnitude, weighing [more] and of a more pleasant taste than [the ones] in England.

Robert Horne, *A Brief Description of the Province of Carolina; Narratives of Early Carolina, 1650–1708*, ed. Alexander Salley Jr. New York: Scribner's, 1911. Early Americas Digital Archive, www.mith2.umd.edu/eada/html/display .php?docs=horne_briefcarolina.xml&action=show.

from New York, Maryland, and other regions to move to Pennsylvania.

The Carolinas

As a commercial center, Philadelphia regularly competed with New York, Baltimore, and Boston. One of its staunchest rivals, however, was Charleston, South Carolina. At first there was only one Carolina—for which King Charles II granted a charter in 1663. The first residents of the new colony arrived in 1670 and established Charles Towne (later modified to Charleston) on the Ashley River. They came mainly from Virginia. But as time went on, others arrived from England's Caribbean colony of Barbados, as well as from Europe. Most were drawn to the region's pleasant climate and rich natural resources. In 1666 one impressed Englishman wrote:

This Province lying so near Virginia, and yet more southward, enjoys the fertility and advantages thereof; and yet is so far distant, as to be freed from the inconstancy of the weather, which is a great cause of [poor health]. Also, being in the latitude of [the pleasant island of Bermuda] may expect the like healthfulness which it has [earlier] enjoyed, and doubtless there is no plantation that ever the English [have found], in all respects so good as this [rich soil in Carolina].[51]

The division of the Carolina colony into two sections was partly inspired by the fact that the northern section differed in terrain and climate from the southern one. Also, the area was so large that transportation and communication within its borders was at first very difficult. As a result, by 1712, the two sections had come to see themselves as separate entities. The official division into North Carolina and South Carolina, by then both crown colonies, came in 1729.

Of the two Carolinas, South Carolina was more populous and commercially successful than its northern namesake for many decades. This was due in large part to the commercial success of Charleston. Ethnically diverse and bustling with activity, it was the fourth busiest port in British America by 1770.

All Americans

Also by the mid-1770s, British America had thirteen populous and prosperous colonies on North America's eastern sea-board. In addition to Massachusetts, New York, Maryland, Virginia, Pennsylvania, and the Carolinas, they included New Hampshire, Rhode Island, Connecticut, New Jersey, Delaware, and Georgia. By 1754, their combined population was about 1.5 million. And by 1775 the population had reached 2.4 million.

The thirteen colonies of America: Massachusetts, New York, Maryland, Virginia, Pennsylvania, North and South Carolina, New Hampshire, Rhode Island, Connecticut, New Jersey, Delaware, and Georgia.

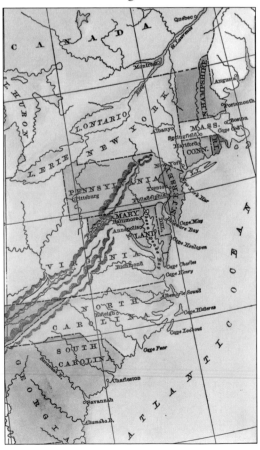

At that juncture, 85 percent of the inhabitants were English, Irish, Welsh, or Scottish (or, collectively speaking, British). The rest were mainly of German, Dutch, Scandinavian, or African descent. Ultimately these distinctions mattered little, for in the following fateful year (1776), the colonists broke away from their mother country and became Americans.

Chapter Seven

CHANGING RELATIONS WITH THE INDIANS

Looking back on the creation and early growth of Britain's North American colonies, one can readily see that much of their success was due to abundant innate skills, a great deal of hard work, and in many cases sheer determination. But one must also concede that their success would have been impossible if the Native American civilization in the region had remained intact. The eastern seaboard was inhabited by numerous Indian tribes when white Europeans first arrived. And the initial question for both whites and Indians was whether there was room there for both peoples.

If the whites had been content to stay put in their small initial colonies on the coasts and had never expanded inland, perhaps the two peoples could have coexisted in peace. Certainly they did enjoy a few years of friendly relations. This was partly because most of the first English settlers badly needed the Indians' help. Often ill prepared, colonists desperately required the natives "to guide and instruct them on survival in the American wilderness," writes University of Oklahoma scholar Arrell M. Gibson. According to Gibson:

> The colonists turned to Indians to teach them planting techniques and culture of crops by which they could sustain themselves and eventually prosper, to hunt furs to enrich their trading establishment, to labor on their plantations, and to serve as colonial troops in various wars Great Britain waged against European adversaries in North America.[52]

Although several native peoples did readily aid the white colonists in various ways, the sad fact (from the Indians' point of view) was that white expansion was inevitable. And the key commodity in that expansion was the land the Indians inhabited. There came a point when the whites felt that the only thing they needed from the natives was that land. And so the Indians suffered what one expert calls "centuries of catastrophic and disruptive cultural change in the face of an inexorable [relentless] European [presence]."[53] In addition to

Settlers often needed Indians to help guide them through unfamiliar American wilderness. One of the most famous guides was Squanto, shown here helping a Pilgrim.

the outright theft of Native American lands, this cultural catastrophe included slaughtering those who resisted; and herding the survivors onto remote reservations. Also, indirectly more Indians died from deadly diseases for which they had no natural resistance.

A Markedly Different Lifestyle

Gibson sums up the eventual English colonial policy toward the Indians as "exploitive and unnecessarily destructive and demeaning."[54] In retrospect, it is natural to ask why the colonists felt justified not only in taking native lands, but also in pursuing a strategy of cruel treatment and in some cases outright extermination. The general answer is that the vast majority of whites viewed the Indians as inferiors and enemies. And in their long history, Europeans had traditionally denounced, tortured, enslaved, and/or killed those seen as inferiors or enemies.

Among the specific reasons why the English and other Europeans saw Indians as inferior to themselves was the major difference in lifestyle between the two peoples. Native Americans did not have many of the material, political, and cultural elements that all Europeans took for granted. These included nation-states and large cities with centralized governments, royal palaces, and permanent uniformed armies; town halls, churches, and other large public buildings; schools, banks, shops, and other community insti-

English colonists mistakenly thought that Native Americans were "uncivilized" and inferior, due to certain Indian dress and traditions.

tutions; large shipbuilding methods and facilities; and metal-smelting techniques and the wide range of metal objects taken for granted in Europe, including cannons and other firearms.

It did not occur to most whites that the Indians did not have these things because they had developed societies that did not need them. Instead, the colonists assumed the Indians lacked these "civilized" refinements because their intelligence, skills, and morals were substandard. Moreover, people with inferior morals could not be trusted or allowed to mingle in white society. One settler described the Indians in the following disparaging manner:

> They have the shapes of men and may be of the human species, but certainly in their present state they approach nearer the character of Devils; take an Indian. . . . Can you trust his word or confide in his promise? When he makes war upon you, when he takes you prisoner . . . will he spare you? . . . On this principle are not the whole Indian nations murderers?[55]

Religious Disparities and Intolerance

Even more important to most whites than the Indians' lack of cities, palaces, shops, and metal artifacts was the fact that they were not Christians. With a few exceptions, the white colonists were Christians who believed in a single, all-powerful god, specifically the one mentioned in the Bible. They were certain that theirs was the only true faith. And they looked on the Indians' beliefs in nature gods and spirits as not only false, but also primitive, childish, and against the "real" god. The colonists therefore

Powhatan's Powerful Words

In a speech to Jamestown leader John Smith, the Algonquin chief whom the colonists called Powhatan questioned the settlers' motives. In retrospect, these words came to reflect the feelings of other Indians who found themselves fighting to preserve their way of life against encroaching white civilization. Powhatan said:

I have seen two generations of my people die [and] I know the difference between peace and war better than any man in my country. I am now grown old, and must die soon. . . . I wish [my people] to know as much as I do, and that your love to them may be like mine to you. Why will you take by force what you may have quietly by love? Why will you destroy us who supply you with food? What can you get by war? We can hide our provisions and run into the woods; then you will starve for wronging your friends. Why are you jealous of us? We are unarmed, and willing to give you what you ask, if you come in a friendly manner, and not so simple as not to know that it is much better to eat good meat, sleep comfortably, live quietly . . . laugh and be merry with the English [than] to run away from them, and to lie cold in the woods, feed on acorns, roots and such trash, and be so hunted that I can neither eat nor sleep.

Quoted in Howard Zinn, *A People's History of the United States.* New York: HarperCollins, 1980, p. 213.

felt morally justified in imposing themselves on Indian society, including the seizure of Native American lands.

Illustrative of this approach was the attitude expressed by the Puritans, which was later echoed by other English groups. According to Gibson:

Puritan rhetoric [oratory] ordained that the Indians' resistance to their law, because it was "God's law," comprised blasphemy [profanity or wickedness in God's sight], the ultimate sin, and thus placed the offending Indians outside the pale of protection and their lands could be taken by force or conquest with impunity.[56]

The fact that the Indians were not Christians also gave many colonists what they saw as both a license and a duty to convert the natives to Christianity. One Boston missionary summed up the intolerant and patronizing attitude of many whites in a speech to the chief of a tribe native to the New York region. He said:

There is but one religion, and but one way to serve God, and if you do not embrace the right way, you cannot be happy hereafter. You have never worshipped the Great Spirit in a manner acceptable to him; but have, all your lives, been in great errors and darkness. To endeavor to remove these errors, and open your eyes, so that you might see clearly, is my business with you.[57]

The wise reply by the chief shows clearly that Indians were not unsophisticated about philosophy and religion, as the missionary had assumed to be the case. The chief responded:

You say that you are right and we are lost. How do you know this to be true? . . . You say there is but one way to worship and serve the Great Spirit. If there is but one religion, why do you white people differ so much about it? . . . We also have a religion. . . . It teaches us to be thankful for all the favors we receive; to love each other, and to be united. We never quarrel about religion.[58]

Despite the logic of the chief's remarks and similar comments made by other Native Americans, most white colonists were unwilling to extend to the Indians the religious tolerance they themselves demanded from the English government. As a result, scholar Philip Kopper writes, many settlers condemned the natives as "hopeless, vicious, and undeserving."[59] And along with white seizures of Indian lands, such attitudes steadily drove a wedge between the two peoples, making bloodshed inevitable.

Annihilating Entire Tribes

The earliest example of open warfare between settlers and Indians was between the colonists of Jamestown

Seeing that colonists were trying to take their land, the Indians retaliated and attacked settlers at the Jamestown colony in 1622, killing more than 350 people.

and the Algonquin tribes that inhabited the areas surrounding it. Some of these tribes were at first friendly and helped the colonists. But this changed in the years following the colony's adoption of tobacco as its primary crop. Because the tobacco sold so well in Europe, the settlers wanted to grow more, which over time necessitated finding new plots of land to cultivate. Subsequently the settlers expanded their colony farther and farther inland, chopping down forests and building farms in areas the Indians had long used for hunting and fishing.

Some Algonquin advocated stopping this encroachment by attacking the colony. But the most powerful chief in the region, Wahunsenacawh, whom the whites called Powhatan, urged them to hold their tempers. First, he said, trade with the colonists had proved advantageous to his people and other local tribes and going to war with the whites would surely end that trade. Secondly, Powhatan was convinced that the settlers would require a total of only a few thousand acres for tobacco cultivation. Because he did not foresee the scope of the white expansion that was to come, he used his influence to keep the peace for as long as he lived.

Following Powhatan's death in 1618, his successors quickly came to realize that he had been wrong—the colonists would not be content with a small slice of coastal territory. Seeing their way of life threatened, the Indians went to war. Led by Powhatan's brother, Opechancanough, they assaulted Jamestown's outlying settlements in the spring of 1622. More than 350 whites were killed, which provoked a counterattack by the rest of the settlers. This was no ordinary military response, however. Feeling betrayed by the Indians, whom they now saw as savages, the colonists implemented an approach that amounted to annihilation of the enemy. In campaign after campaign, they destroyed entire native villages; butchered the residents, including women and children; and burned any Indian crops they found. In time they captured and killed Opechancanough and slew all but a thousand of the local Algonquin. These survivors signed a treaty with the whites in 1646. It allotted them a small parcel of land, one of the first Indian reservations in North America, on which to live under English rule and colonial law.

A similar eradication of an entire tribe occurred farther north, in what is now Connecticut, in the 1630s. Tensions had been rising for some time between various Indian groups in coastal Connecticut and Rhode Island and whites from Plymouth and Massachusetts Bay who had been settling in these areas. In 1636 violence erupted between the settlers and a local tribe, the Pequot. During the initial fighting, some thirty whites were killed, and the Indians kidnapped several others. In retaliation, a combined force of settlers from nearly all the New England colonies converged on the Pequot, killed most of them, and enslaved the survivors. Puritan leader Increase Mather's reaction typified most colonists' feelings about this near genocide. He said, "We thank thee, Lord, that on this day we have sent six hundred heathen souls to hell!"[60]

A Policy of Extermination

Thus, over the course of only a few years, most colonists came to view Indians not as friendly helpers but as bloodthirsty savages who must be destroyed. Summing up the new attitude, one modern expert writes that the vast majority of colonists

> conveniently concluded that their Indian neighbors were committed in their heathenism [non-Christian beliefs], were hopeless of redemption, and were thus an obstacle to the advance of "superior" European Christian civilization. The sooner they were destroyed the better, and harassment and extermination became a conscious policy [of white settlers].[61]

This stark change occurred in every colony, eventually even in the usually tolerant and fair-minded Pennsylvania. As long as the Quakers were in charge of that colony, relations with the natives remained largely nonviolent. But in 1726 the Quakers lost control of the local legislature. After that, fear and hatred of Indians steadily took hold in those sections of society in which it did not already exist. And the government created a law that offered $130, then a great deal of money, for an adult male Indian scalp. The scalp of an adult female Indian went for 50 dollars.

Farther south, in the Carolinas, the colonists skillfully played one Indian group against another. In the late 1600s settlers supplied members of a coastal tribe, the Yamasee, with guns and sent them inland to hunt deer and capture other Indians who would then be sold in Charleston's slave markets. In 1708 South Carolina had about fourteen hundred Indian slaves who sold for an average of twenty English pounds apiece. (That was only about half of what a black slave sold for, mainly because Indian

Colonists who viewed Indians as savages brutally wiped out Indian tribes across New England.

The First Indian Reservations

In the following extract, University of Oklahoma scholar Arrell M. Gibson describes the creation of the first Indian "reservations" in Massachusetts in the 1600s.

Christian plantations for New England Indians began at Natick in 1651, when the Massachusetts General Court created an 8,000-acre reservation for the tiny Nonantum tribe. The following year [the court] passed the first allotment act. Indian residents of this plantation, after demonstrating that they could live "civilly and orderly" received an individual allotment of land for farming and stock raising. . . . Natick Indians, with the help of colonial carpenters, constructed English-style residences on their allotments. Between 1650 and 1670, [the court] created several additional reservations. To manage this growing system of Indian reservations, the General Court in 1656 established the office of superintendent of Indian affairs for Massachusetts, who was to direct the "civilization" process for the Christian plantation residents.

Arrell M. Gibson, *The American Indian: Prehistory to the Present.* Lexington, MA: D.C. Heath, 1980, pp. 192–93.

captives tended to be more unruly and tried to escape more often.) Justifying the enslavement of Indians, one Carolinian said, "It both serves to lessen their number before the French can arm them and it is a more effective way of civilizing and instructing [them]."[62]

In time, the Yamasee, too, became victims of this arrogant and callous attitude. As the white population of the Carolinas grew, new settlers demanded the right to take Yamasee lands. And when the Yamasee objected, the alliance between them and the colony dissolved. A full-blown war erupted in 1715. Although the native warriors fought valiantly and managed to kill more than two hundred settlers, they were grossly outnumbered and outgunned. So they had no real chance. After several years of intermittent fighting, only about twenty Yamasee were left alive out of a population of approximately five thousand.

An Incalculable Debt

Similar scenarios played out across the eastern seaboard in the years that followed. And by the end of the colonial era, the thirteen British colonies, soon to become American states, were largely free of what their inhabitants perceived as the Indian "menace." This made the creation of a new nation populated principally by whites possible.

That nation was destined to become the strongest and freest on Earth. Eventually its government outlawed slavery and discrimination, and its people rejected racism and other ills of the past. Many of its citizens also found the courage and decency to admit that much of the country's success was built on Native American losses. "North American history is just as much the story of a displacement of a people as it is that of European expansion,"[63] writes Carl Waldman, a noted chronicler of the Indians. As he and other modern observers point out, it is too late to restore all of the native lands that were taken. But it will never be too late to acknowledge the incalculable debt the United States owes to the Indians of its colonial and later eras.

Notes

Introduction: Creating New and Exceptional Societies

1. Herbert Applebaum, *The American Work Ethic and the Changing Work Force: A Historical Perspective.* Westport, CT: Greenwood, 1998, p. 15.
2. Alan Taylor, *American Colonies: The Settling of North America.* New York: Penguin, 2001, p. xi.
3. Taylor, *American Colonies,* p. xii.
4. Vincent N. Parrillo, *Diversity in America.* Thousand Oaks, CA: Forge, 2009, p. 45.

Chapter One: The Native Americans Before Colonization

5. Quoted in Richard Kavesh, blog, "Rethinking Columbus: Great Explorer or Greedy Conqueror?" Rapid City Journal, October 11, 2008, http://blogs.rapidcityjournal.com/indigenous_pov/?p=30.
6. Philip Kopper, *The Smithsonian Book of North American Indians.* New York: Abrams, 1986, pp. 31, 33.
7. Kathleen Bragdon, "Massachusett," in *Encyclopedia of North American Indians,* ed. Frederick E. Hoxie. Boston: Houghton Mifflin, 1996, p. 362.

8. Quoted in Hoxie, *Encyclopedia of North American Indians.* pp. 680–81.
9. Quoted in Arrell M. Gibson, *The American Indian: Prehistory to the Present.* Lexington, MA: D.C. Heath, 1980, p. 250.

Chapter Two: The First Europeans to See North America

10. Taylor, *American Colonies,* p. 24.
11. Irwin Unger, *These United States: The Questions of Our Past.* Boston: Little, Brown, 2002, p. 5.
12. Christopher Columbus, "Christopher Columbus: Extracts from Journal," Internet Medieval Sourcebook, www.fordham.edu/halsall/source/columbus1.html.
13. Columbus, "Christopher Columbus."
14. H.P. Biggar, ed., *The Precursors of Jacques Cartier 1497–1534: A Collection of Documents Relating to the Early History of the Dominion of Canada.* Ottawa, Canada: Government Printing Bureau, 1911, pp. 7–10. http://tudorplace.com.ar/Documents/CabotHenryVIIpatent.htm.

15. Quoted in Lawrence C. Wroth, ed., *The Voyages of Giovanni da Verrazzano, 1524–1528.* New Haven, CT: Yale University Press, 1970, pp. 136–37.
16. Quoted in Gabriel Archer, *Gosnold's Settlement at Cuttyhunk.* Boston: Old South Work, 1902, pp. 5–6.

Chapter Three: The Colonizers and Their Motives

17. Quoted in David F. Hawke, *Everyday Life in Early America.* New York: Harper and Row, 1989, p. 2.
18. William Bradford, *Bradford's History of Plymouth Plantation,* ed. William T. Davis. New York: Scribner's, 1908. www.mith2.umd.edu/eada/html/display.php?docs=bradford_history.xml&action=show.
19. Howard S. Russell, *A Long, Deep Furrow: Three Centuries of Farming in New England.* Hanover, NH: University Press of New England, 1976, p. 28.
20. Unger, *These United States,* p. 27.
21. Hawke, *Everyday Life in Early America,* p. 2.
22. Samuel E. Morison, *The Oxford History of the American People: Vol. 1, Prehistory to 1789.* New York: Plume, 1994, p. 102.
23. Unger, *These United States,* p. 37.
24. Quoted in Edwin M. Bacon, ed., *English Voyages of Adventure and Discovery,* Retold from Hakluyt. New York: Scribner's 1908, p. 3.
25. Quoted in A.S. Salley, ed., *Records of the Secretary of the Province and the Register of the Province of South Carolina, 1671–1675.* Columbia: Historical Commission of South Carolina, 1944, pp. 7–8.
26. Hawke, *Everyday Life in Early America,* p. 4.

Chapter Four: Establishment of Roanoke and Jamestown

27. John C. Miller, *The First Frontier: Life in Colonial America.* Lanham, MD: University Press of America, 1986, p. 15.
28. Ralph Lane, *Discourse on the First Colony,* in *Capt. John Smith: Writings, with Other Narratives of Roanoke, Jamestown, and the First English Settlement of America,* ed. James Horn. New York: Library of America, 2007, pp. 838–39.
29. John White, *Narrative of the 1590 Voyage,* in *Capt. John Smith,* pp. 914–15.
30. Taylor, *American Colonies,* pp. 124–25.
31. Quoted in Samuel Purchas, *Hakluytus Posthumas,* vol. 19. Glasgow, Scotland: MacLehose, 1903, p. 58.
32. Taylor, *American Colonies,* p. 131.
33. Morison, *Oxford History of the American People,* p. 89.
34. James Horn, *A Land as God Made It: Jamestown and the Birth of America.* New York: Basic, 2006, p. 290.

Chapter Five: Founding Plymouth and Massachusetts Bay

35. John Smith, *A Description of New England*, in Capt. John Smith, pp. 137, 149.
36. Quoted in Robert A. Peterson, "The Pilgrims in Holland," November 1988, *Freeman*. www.theadvocates.org/freeman/8811petr.html.
37. William Bradford, *Of Plymouth Plantation, 1620–1647*, ed. Samuel E. Morison. New York: Knopf, 1952, p. 25.
38. Quoted in Anonymous, "A Relation or Journal of the Proceedings of the Plantation Settled at Plymouth in New England," in *Mourt's Relation: A Journal of the Pilgrims at Plymouth*, ed. Dwight B. Heath. Carlisle, MA: Applewood, 1963, p. 45.
39. Bradford, *Of Plymouth Plantation*, pp. 38–39.
40. Bradford, *Of Plymouth Plantation*, p. 253.
41. Quoted in Merrill Jensen, ed., *American Colonial Documents to 1776*. New York: Oxford University Press, 1955, p. 147.
42. Miller, *First Frontier*, p. 43.
43. Miller, *First Frontier*, p. 55.
44. Morison, *Oxford History of the American People*, pp. 73–74.

Chapter Six: The Mid-Atlantic and Southern Colonies

45. Morison, *Oxford History of the American People*, p. 75.
46. Quoted in New Netherland Museum and the *Half Moon*, "The History of New Netherland and the Half Moon," New Netherland Museum and the Half Moon. www.newnetherland.org/history.html.
47. George Alsop, *A Character of the Province of Maryland*, ed. Newton D. Mereness. Cleveland, OH: Burrows, 1902. www.mith2.umd.edu/eada/html/display.php?docs=alsop_character.xml&action=show.
48. Quoted in Clayton C. Hall, ed., *Narratives of Early Maryland*. New York: Scribner's, 1910, pp. 85–86.
49. Taylor, *American Colonies*, p. 267.
50. Quoted in Samuel M. Janny, *The Life of William Penn*. Philadelphia: Lippincott, Grambo, 1852, p. 179.
51. Robert Horne, *A Brief Description of the Province of Carolina: Narratives of Early Carolina, 1650–1708*, ed. Alexander Salley Jr. New York: Scribner's, 1911. www.mith2.umd.edu/eada/html/display.php?docs=horne_briefcarolina.xml&action=show.

Chapter Seven: Changing Relations with the Indians

52. Gibson, *The American Indian*, p. 186.
53. Brian M. Fagan, *Ancient North America*. New York: Thames and Hudson, 2005, p. 511.
54. Gibson, *American Indian*, p. 186.
55. Quoted in Wilcomb E. Washburn, ed., *The Indian and the White Man*. Garden City, NY: Doubleday, 1964, p. 116.

56. Gibson, *The American Indian*, p. 190.
57. Quoted in Washburn, *The Indian and the White Man*, p. 210.
58. Quoted in Washburn, *The Indian and the White Man*, pp. 212–13.
59. Kopper, *The Smithsonian Book of North American Indians*, p. 277.
60. Quoted in Alnoba Waubunaki, "With the Passing of Puritanism the Red Man Comes," *Quarterly Journal of the Society of American Indians 2,* 1914, p. 123.
61. Gibson, *The American Indian*, p. 209.
62. Quoted in Charles Hudson, *The Southeastern Indians.* Knoxville: University of Tennessee Press, 1976, p. 438.
63. Carl Waldman, *Atlas of the North American Indian.* New York: Facts On File, 1985, p. 165.

Time Line

B.C.

ca. 15,000–ca. 11,000
Bands of hunter-gatherers from what is now Siberia migrate into North America, becoming the Native Americans.

ca. 3300–3000
The Sumerians build the world's first cities near the Persian Gulf, in Mesopotamia.

ca. 1000
Farming becomes common among numerous Native American tribes.

ca. 753
Rome is founded in western Italy.

A.D.

ca. 985
Viking explorers sight Newfoundland and possibly Cape Cod.

1347
The bubonic plague, also called the Black Death, ravages Europe.

1497
Five years after Christopher Columbus's famous voyage to the Caribbean region, English explorer John Cabot reaches North America.

1517
German clergyman Martin Luther instigates the Reformation, in which Protestant groups break away from the Catholic Church.

1524
Italian navigator Giovanni da Verrazano explores what is now New York Harbor.

1564
Noted Italian Renaissance painter, sculptor, and architect Michelangelo dies.

1585
English settlers land on Roanoke Island, in what is now North Carolina.

1588
The English defeat the huge fleet of warships known as the Spanish Armada.

1607
After the Roanoke colonists mysteriously disappear, another English expedition establishes the Jamestown Colony in Virginia.

1620
Separatists from England create a colony at Plymouth, in what is now Massachusetts.

1625
Dutch settlers establish the town of New Amsterdam (later New York City) on Manhattan Island.

1648
Shah Jahan, emperor of India, erects the magnificent Taj Mahal as a monument to his deceased wife.

1670
English settlers establish Charleston, in what is now South Carolina.

1729
England's Carolina province splits into North Carolina and South Carolina.

1762
Catherine II (also known as Catherine the Great) becomes ruler of Russia.

1776
Britain's thirteen North American colonies declare their independence and the American Revolution begins.

For More Information

Books

Bernard Bailyn, *The Peopling of British North America: An Introduction*. New York: Vintage, 1988. This book is a well-written overview of the various individuals and groups involved in creating the British colonies.

James Deetz and Patricia S. Deetz, *The Times of Their Lives: Life, Love, and Death in Plymouth Colony*. New York: Anchor, 2001. The authors of this book are first-rate scholars who present a fresh, compelling, and well-documented look at the real history of Plymouth Colony.

Brian M. Fagan, *Ancient North America*. New York: Thames and Hudson, 2005. This is an excellent, highly detailed study of precontact North American Indians, broken down by geographic region.

Arrell M. Gibson, *The American Indian: Prehistory to the Present*. Lexington, MA: D.C. Heath, 1980. This is an information-packed overview of Native American peoples, with a useful section on their earliest settlements.

David F. Hawke, *Everyday Life in Early America*. New York: Harper and Row, 1989. This is a well-written exploration of early colonial life, including farms, houses, health, race relations, and manners and morals.

James Horn, ed., *Capt. John Smith: Writings, with Other Narratives of Roanoke, Jamestown, and the First English Settlement of America*. New York: Library of America, 2007. This is a huge and useful collection of original documents by some of the major explorers and colonial leaders who helped to shape British colonial America. Highly recommended.

Peter C. Mancall and James H. Merrill, eds., *American Encounters: Natives and Newcomers from European Contact to Indian Removal, 1500–1850*. New York: Routledge, 2000. This is an excellent collection of essays by noted historians and other experts about the destruction of Native American civilization.

John C. Miller, *The First Frontier: Life in Colonial America*. Lanham, MD: University Press of America, 1986. This book offers a very thoughtful and useful look at life and customs in colonial America, featuring numerous colorful primary source quotations.

Alan Taylor, *American Colonies: The Settling of North America*. New York: Penguin, 2001. This is an extremely well-researched book about the colonies, written by a Pulitzer Prize–winning scholar.

Internet Sources

Roger F. Dowd, "The Pequot War," Roger Dowd Design, www.dowdgen.com/dowd/document/pequots.html.

National Park Service, "Dutch Colonies," National Park Service, www.nps.gov/history/NR/travel/kingston/colonization.htm.

Web Sites

Early Americas Digital Archive (www.mith2.umd.edu/eada). This site offers a collection of electronic texts originally written in or about the Americas from 1492 to approximately 1820.

Colonial Williamsburg: That the Future May Learn From the Past–Kids Zone (http://www.history.org/kids/). A kid-focused site that helps teach what daily life was like in colonial Williamsburg. Also includes parent and teacher activities.

The Plymouth Colony Archive Project (www.histarch.uiuc.edu/plymouth). This site focuses on colonial times in the Plymouth Colony. It includes biographies, court records and laws, maps, and much more.

Index

Virginia Company, 47

Picture Credits

About the Author

Historian and award-winning author Don Nardo has written many books for young adults about American history, among them *The Salem Witch Trials*; *The Sons of Liberty*; *The Declaration of Independence*; *The Mexican-American War*; *The Great Depression*; biographies of presidents Thomas Jefferson, Andrew Johnson, and Franklin D. Roosevelt; several volumes about native American history and culture; and a survey of the weapons and tactics of the American Revolution. Nardo lives with his wife, Christine, in Massachusetts.